Living Proof

Celebrating the Gifts that Came
Wrapped in Sandpaper

Presented by

Lisa Nichols

Yinspire Media
info@yinspiremedia.com
www.YinspireMedia.com

Presented by: Lisa Nichols

Producer: Ruby Yeh

Editorial Director: AJ Harper

Print Management: Book Lab

Cover Design: Pearl Planet Design

Book Design & Typesetting: Chinook Design, Inc.

ISBN-13: 978–09819708-7-5

Printed in the United States of America

Contents

Lisa Nichols

Introduction

Our lives are living proof of the human spirit. We are all examples of the choice to stand, no matter what, to lead, no matter what, to believe, *no matter what.*

We demonstrate the resiliency of humankind every day when we choose to get back up, when we choose to love again, when we choose to trust again, to believe again, to forgive ourselves again. And it is in these supreme acts of faith that we become the living proof of what is possible.

In this, my first anthology since *Chicken Soup for the African American Woman's Soul,* I celebrate the unshakeable, unbreakable, indestructible power that is the human spirit. I chose to title the book *Living Proof* after reading the more than thirty-five transformational true stories of ordinary people who made the extraordinary decision to believe again, in spite of their circumstances. The co-authors of this book truly are living, breathing examples of faith, resiliency and the human spirit.

I have met every author in this book; most at a conference, or at one of my workshops. Each one of them wore a stylish outfit and carried beautiful business cards, and each one of them spoke with passion about their hopes and dreams. Little did I know that they had fought for their lives. Little did I know that some of them endured tremendous suffering—in the killing fields of Cambodia, in hospital waiting rooms and in their own bedrooms; at the hands of lovers, spouses, parents and strangers; by choice or by a twist of fate. Little did I know that some were once so sick, so lonely and so heartbroken, they had lost their will to live.

And, little did I know how much joy, success and sheer beauty they created for themselves and for others—improving the quality of life for residents in long-term care living environments; building schools; advocating for children with special needs; and, through their coaching, speaking, writing and training, helping people find and live in their own authentic power.

In reading their stories, I was overcome with admiration for each and every one of them. As I turned each page I was right there with them, holding my breath, gasping in surprise, my heart beating faster as I wondered, "Could I have done that? *Would* I have done that? How is she going to get out of this?"

I am honored that these amazing co-authors have chosen to share their stories with me, and I'm excited to be with them again now that I know the depth of their core beings.

You don't really know the truth and scope of someone's journey, you don't know how high the mountain they've had to climb or how deep the valley they've had to get out of in order to stand beside you. People look at my life now and see a bestselling author, an international speaker, someone with a bit of celebrity status. But when I look at my own story, I see the little girl in South Central Los Angeles, wondering if she'll ever know a safe day. I see the struggling student who rarely earned above a C in school. I see the young mother who wrapped her baby boy in a towel for two days because she couldn't afford to buy diapers.

When I look at the woman I had to become in order to transform the life I was living, all I can say is, I am living proof. When I recognized that every single experience happened so that I could be the woman I am today, I saw that some of my greatest challenges were my greatest blessings. Some of my best gifts came wrapped in sandpaper; came wrapped in tears; came wrapped in bumps, bruises, humiliation and shame. I didn't understand it at the time, but when I got still and allowed myself to breathe again, I looked back at each of the obstacles, dilemmas and losses that *could have* taken me down and asked the right question: What was the blessing of that experience?

When I stopped asking, "Why me?" and started asking, "Why *not* me?" I was able to share my own living-proof stories of resilience, reinvention and redemption.

The stories in this book will inspire you, encourage you and remind you that you are greater than your experiences. It would have meant the world to me to read this book in my darkest moments—it means the world to me *now*. But to have held this

---

What I love about the human spirit is, if one person has access to it, we all do.

---

book in my hands all those years ago, when I felt powerless and afraid, to have had the privilege of reading these living, breathing examples of ordinary people choosing to lead extraordinary lives, would have given me the hope I did not have and so desperately needed.

These stories are *living proof* that whatever you may be going through, the darkness is only temporary—it's not your destiny. This book is proof that you are greater than your circumstances, whatever they are. You have an opportunity to turn a test into your testimony; to turn a mountain into your platform; to turn the challenges that would break you into reasons you sing, write, speak, teach; and, like the co-authors in this book, offer up *your* story as living proof of what is possible.

I am proud, *so proud* of the co-authors who told me their stories and then courageously shared them with you and the world. Let their stories remind you that everything you need is already in you; that you are enough and you have always been enough; and that no matter how ugly it gets, you are destined for greatness.

What I love about the human spirit is, if one person has access to it, we all do. Our lives are living proof of the magnitude and resiliency of the human spirit. *Your* life is living proof of the human spirit. So as you read this book, celebrate the champion you have been in the past, the champion you are today and the champion you will become.

Dr. Julie Thong

The Smell of Grass

*B*ang! Bang! Bang! "Hey, @#%^&! You must leave your home right now!" a soldier yelled, pointing his gun toward my mother's face. "Take only three days' worth of belongings!" The Communist soldiers screamed, raging while shooting their guns up into the sky to force people to leave their hometown.

It happened on April 17, 1975, without warning: Khmer Rouge soldiers popped up everywhere in Cambodia, dressed like ninjas in their black uniforms with red-checked scarves and AK-47s. They swarmed into our town, Battambang, at precisely noon. The troops marched into City Hall, where my father worked as a Secretary of the Province. Helicopters landed in front of his office to rescue government officials. Many climbed aboard, but my father refused. "I have a wife and eight children to protect." He rushed home just in time to save us. I was the oldest of the eight children and had just turned fifteen during that time. In my panic, I moved quickly to help my parents.

We were forced out of Battambang with only three days' worth of food and clothing. After two days of trudging, we ended up in a rice field that was full of thorns, bushes and dragonflies. No one could sleep that night because of the gunshots and the sounds of coyotes, frogs, crickets and snakes. We were sheltered under a tree that was full of bees and ticks. Being bitten and stung by all those bugs, my siblings were scared and crying. We were all horrified, hungry, tired and thirsty. We met some people who were kind to us, and shared their food with us.

The Khmer Rouge soldiers killed many people they thought were educated. We wept together when we heard that a family we knew had been killed because the father had a prestigious position and the children were all educated. My father told us that we had to change our names and keep our backgrounds secret to protect our identities and our lives, or we would be next. We had to pretend we were peasant farmers.

My real name, Khanteya, means "patience" and "determination." My farmer's name was Bo Rie, which means "beautiful rice." Even though Bo Rie was the name I used for the next four years, the intensity of my experience over that time proved that my real name *was* patience and determination.

Because people recognized my father, we kept moving from village to village. Our walk across the rice fields was very treacherous. The sharp rice stems scratched and scraped our skin; the muddy water was full of leeches and snails. We came across a

---

Each day, we got just a spoonful of rice to eat. I always ate a few grains and saved some for later.

---

family my father had helped while he was in power. They helped protect us and taught us how to live like poor farmers. A few days later, my siblings and I were separated from our parents and sent to concentration camps, where we were segregated according to age and sex.

Each day, we got just a spoonful of rice to eat. I always ate a few grains and saved some for later. I spent my days planting rice, digging and building water channels for the Communists. At night, we slept on the cold ground in rows, like sardines in a can. The soldiers stood guard over us, brandishing their AK-47s. I held my breath every time they walked by; girls who talked too much or were found to be from the city would be raped and shot. They would poke their gun barrels at the knee of the girl they suspected and drag her away to the rice field. Every day I lived in fear; every night, I wondered if it was my turn.

One night, I slept next to a girl named Sokha. She was so hungry, she often whispered in my ear about her favorite foods. The guards heard her and tapped her on the knee. Her body jerked, and touched my knee. I thought it was my turn to be marched into

The smell of the grass woke me up. I remembered I was not a body to be used up and thrown away.

the rice field. My blood ran cold. My heart was pounding. I couldn't help feeling nauseated, and started peeing in my pants. Sokha got up and moved slowly, with a horrified look. At that moment, I realized it was my friend they wanted, not me. She kept looking at me, wanting to say good-bye. I had to pretend I didn't see her, or they would have taken me as well. They marched her to the rice field, raped her first and then shot her. Sokha is not forgotten.

In my second year at the concentration camp, I became very ill. Every joint was seriously swollen and painful. I couldn't walk. I moved by crawling. I lost all my hair and weighed about sixty pounds. The soldiers dragged me to the killing ground, dumped me on top of a pile of bodies and left me to die. Some people in the pile weren't completely dead. I felt their fingers and toes moving. They weren't strong enough to fight. They were exhausted by their ordeals and preferred to die quietly. I prayed that my own death would not come swiftly, and that I would find my parents. I became weaker, and then collapsed.

I woke up the next morning with the sun beaming sharply on my face. I slowly squinted. I was too fatigued to move or even sit up. It took every ounce of strength and determination I had just to roll over. I scooted across the pile of bodies, moving one leg at a time, and finally my body reached ground level.

And then my nose hit the grass. My olfactory system came alive. The smell of the grass woke me up. I remembered I was not a body to be used up and thrown away. I was loved. Suddenly, I felt hope. My fear no longer controlled me.

The smell of grass made me hungry, and I began to gobble up the grass like a cow. I chewed the grass, swallowed the dirt, ate ants, bugs and anything else that moved. The grass gave me energy. I was terribly thirsty, and had to crawl on the ground to find water to drink. I saw water buffalo hoofprints, and because it had rained recently, water lay puddled in them. The water was muddy and full of parasites, but I didn't care. I drank from one hoofprint, and moved to the next and drank more.

The water invigorated me, and for the first time in months, I learned how to stand up again. I was shaky and unbalanced, like a newborn foal. I had to practice walking. For a couple of weeks I stayed in that area, eating more grass, drinking more muddy water from the hoofprints and practicing my walking. I decided I was strong enough to start looking for my parents—and off I went. I had no idea where I was going, so I just started walking. The only clothing I had was the faded black pajama-like outfit the Communists had forced all of us to wear. Mine was dirty and full of holes. The sky was vast and blue as the ocean, and the sun beat down on me without mercy. I kept walking.

Normally, the Communist soldiers were everywhere—on every street corner, patrolling every country road, spying on people, making sure no one was running away or leaving their shack. As I walked, the soldiers were nowhere to be found. It was a miracle.

It rained extremely hard, and the road was very muddy and slippery. I kept slipping and falling. My torn clothes were now muddier and hung heavily on my skeletal body. The next night there was a full moon, and I walked past a cemetery, but I wasn't scared. I kept telling myself that my parents were still alive and that I would find them soon. Then, in the distance, I saw a village. There were shacks with roofs made of palm leaves. I had no idea where I was or what village that was, but still I walked to it. I kept walking...

I reached the village, amazed by how much it resembled the village where I last saw my parents. I walked in the direction of where their shack would be. It was sunup, and people were preparing to go work. Amazed, I saw my parents walking out of their shack. "Mom, Dad." They turned and saw me and, thinking I was a ghost, ran away. I called again. Dad turned around and, finally, recognized me. "Wait, Mother," he said. "It looks and sounds like

> *Through all of this, the smell of the grass stayed with me.*

our daughter." I said, "It is me. I escaped." They immediately pulled me into their shack and hid me in their mosquito netting. "Don't do or say anything all day," they said. "Just wait here quietly. If they hear you, they'll kill us all." There was no time for emotions, just survival.

As I lay in the mosquito netting on a bed made of jagged bamboo, I spent my days thinking about the fun times I had as a child. I thought about the games I used to play with my friends, my favorite dishes, the pond in front of our house, and how I used to sneak into my parents' bedroom and listen to The Beatles and Joan Baez songs. Imagining my life before the Communists took over gave me a sense of hope and freedom.

I spent a few painful weeks lying immobile in the shack. Then Vietnamese Communists invaded Cambodia and defeated the Khmer Rouge. They disbanded the concentration camps and allowed people to reunite with their families. One by one my siblings returned home, except my youngest sister, who had died of starvation at six years old. Each sibling had his or her own story to tell.

Once the family was reunited, we eventually crossed over landmine-laden fields and escaped to a refugee camp in Thailand. Through all of this, the smell of the grass stayed with me.

After being sponsored by an American citizen, my family and I were settled in California. Years later, I searched for that smell of grass in hundreds of perfume bottles. Every time I went into a department store, I would test every last bottle.

A few years ago, I was educated about balancing mind, body and spirit through eating habits, exercise, supplements and essential oils. I used many different essential oils, and then one day, in a tiny amber bottle, I found the missing link—an aroma that resonated the smell of grass. I have had many miracles in my life. I have survived hunger and depression, I have found love in the least likely of places, and I have experienced success beyond my imagination. All of that has been possible because of the one scent I gained through my olfactory system: a sense of love, hope, health, happiness, faith, forgiveness and freedom.

Dr. Julie Thong is a dynamic speaker, inspirational author, heartfelt philanthropist, successful entrepreneur, life-changing consultant and corporate health and wellness coach. She teaches how the same strategies she used in a daring escape from the Cambodian Communist regime helped her achieve great health, time and freedom, and create amazing opportunities. She shares how anyone can overcome stress, obstacles, hardship and fear through psychoneurology and aromatherapy.

Dr. Julie is the author of Khanteya: My Quest for Love and Freedom *and* The Power of FEAR: Face Everything And Rejoice. *She co-authored* The Heart of Success *with Joyce Schwarz and is the founder of Amazing Mission International for H.E.A.R.T. (Humanity, Ecology, Art, Recreation & Technology, www.ami4HEART.org) in support of www.CambodiaWeCare. org and other projects around the world. Connect with Dr. Julie Thong via www.JulieThong.com and email to info@JulieThong.com.*

Dame DC Cordova

Meeting Fidel Castro

I n 1979, during the Cold War between the Communist world and the Western world, I set my intention to meet Fidel Castro. I had no idea how I would get an audience with him—he was, after all, the world's most notorious dictator. But I was out to prove something to myself—that the transformational principles I studied and adopted as a way of life really worked.

The idea came to me after studying proven business methods and metaphysical principles at the original Burklyn Business School for Entrepreneurs, which later evolved into our current Excellerated Business School® for Entrepreneurs.

I learned that my job, my *calling*, was to create transformational environments where people could find those gifts within them that may have been hidden their whole lives—while learning entrepreneurship, clearing any blocks they may have had to creating their ideal career or business and, through their success, adding value to humanity.

"What would be the hardest thing to manifest?" I asked some of my closest friends. After a moment I blurted out, "Let's create meeting Fidel Castro." Many laughed and said, "Forget about it. We could never meet Castro. You're such a dreamer." At this time, the Cold War was escalating, and it truly seemed like the "hardest thing" to create, but the "impossibility" of it was the main reason I wanted to go for it. That, and I couldn't think of *anyone* I feared meeting more than Castro. When I was a child in Chile, Fidel Castro was *the* bad guy—you couldn't find anyone worse than him on the planet. I grew up hearing stories about how he tortured people, wouldn't allow them to leave the country and wanted all of the Americas to be Socialist.

I was twelve years old when we moved to the United States, and I remember, in vivid detail, hiding under tables at school for bomb drills during the Cuban missile crisis in 1962—as if hiding under tables would help us in an actual nuclear attack. My head tucked between my knees, my heart racing a mile a minute, I

I was out to prove something to myself—that the transformational principles I studied and adopted as a way of life really worked.

---

was consumed with the most intense fear I had ever experienced; I can still see the cold, green-tiled floor beneath me. *Will they bomb us today? Will Castro help the Russians invade the United States? If they bomb us at school, how will I find my mother?*

Chile, my beloved, safe, magical homeland, seemed a million miles away. And because the threat of war with the Soviet Union was so very real and terrifying, its newly constructed military bases, though more than three thousand miles away on Cuban soil, seemed to be just down the street.

Could I really overcome all "obstacles"—including my own fears—to make the meeting happen? Determined, I set my intention and used the many tools I had been taught: visualization; clearing blocks to the creation of my intentions; working on my fear of really doing big things; doing market research; learning all I could about him; watching him on the news and asking people questions about him. I imagined carrying a banker's box full of books about the new ways of thinking that were becoming so popular in the United States. I wanted to give him the gift of education, to help create peace between the two embattled nations. Castro became part of my consciousness. Every chance I had, I told people, "I'm going to meet Fidel Castro."

Four years later, I was still saying it. While attending a seminar, I told its leaders and the group, "I'm going to meet Fidel Castro. It's in process." I was so sure of myself, as if my bags were packed and my appointment secure, but I still had no clear path to meeting him.

One of my mentors, Bill Galt—the founder of the famous Good Earth Restaurants and a great humanitarian—heard me share my vision and walked over to me. "You never told me you wanted to meet Castro," he said, his eyes dancing. "I know people who know him." *What? He knows people who KNOW Castro?* "My God, Bill, I've told everyone. Why didn't I think of

---

Deep down in my consciousness, I considered Castro a killer.

---

telling you before? I want to be an 'ambassador' of our new style of education, to introduce him to the techniques we use. And maybe this act of kindness will further peace between the United States and Cuba." Bill didn't laugh. He didn't tell me I was crazy. He simply said, "I will call you the moment there's a possibility we can meet him."

I was excited beyond belief, but worried I would get in serious trouble—or worse—if I traveled to Cuba without permission. "It has to be legal, and okay for us to go," I asserted. Bill agreed. I didn't hear from him for many months, and eventually forgot about telling him my plan. I joined a six-month program doing major work to clear my blocks to creation, and began to remember all my fears. *Do I really want to see Fidel Castro? What if everyone is right? What if my idea really IS crazy?*

Deep down in my consciousness, I considered Castro a killer. Meeting him was the scariest thing I could think to do—did I really have to go to such extremes to prove I could create my own reality? Then, I found out that Castro loved education, and that in Cuba they trained doctors to work in what were then called "Third World" countries (where other doctors would not go). Very few people in America knew about this humanitarian activity. Awareness of it shifted my perception of Castro a bit, and I opened up again. *Maybe you can just give him a little bit of light,* I thought.

Then, one Tuesday night in April, 1984, I received a phone call from Bill. "We're on," he said. "We have the possibility of meeting with Castro." My heart leapt, as if ready to fly right out of my chest. "You have to be in Miami by tomorrow night so we can be on a plane to Havana on Thursday. Are you ready?" *Am I ready? Am I ready to meet the biggest, meanest, most ruthless dictator of our time?* "Absolutely," I said. By noon the next day, I was on a flight to Miami.

On the plane, I sat next to Bill and he explained how the possibility of meeting Castro had occurred. "We are guests of Mr. Edward Lamb." Mr. Lamb had gone to the United Nations, and put the word out that anyone who might want to meet Castro could go with him. In the 1950s, Mr. Lamb had been one of the richest men in the United States and a self-described Socialist. In 1969, he saw that the Cuban people were starving as a result of U.S. sanctions and decided to save the sugar industry for Castro.

"He's dying of cancer, DC," Bill told me. "It is his intention to sit across from Castro and appeal to him one more time that it is time to lay down arms and make friends with the United States."

Moments later, Mr. Lamb came back from the first-class cabin to talk with us. A dying man on a mission, he looked ill but had a strong presence. "You know that, officially, the United States and Cuba do not have diplomatic relations," he said to us. "So there's a chance you could be arrested, charged with a felony and put in Federal prison in Georgia." Speechless, I gulped, my heart in my throat. "You are going at your own risk. But know that I am a very rich man, and I will use all of my resources to defend you—and put it in my will." I could see the truth in his eyes, and vowed to press on and take the risk. *I'm so close. I can't turn back now.*

Mr. Lamb went on. "We are the first set of Americans in many, many years who will visit with Castro. He has actually missed visiting with Americans. He enjoyed their company when he studied in the United States." Later, one of the people in our small group said, "The CIA could murder us and blame Castro to create an international incident."

That night, as I lay awake on my hotel bed in Miami, I thought, *This may be my last night on this earth. I could be killed.* Then,

---

I could see the truth in his eyes and vowed to press on and take the risk. I'm so close. I can't turn back now.

---

courage began to build inside of me, and I heard a voice say, "This is what you've been preparing for. This is the thing you will do that will change your life *within* forever."

At the Miami airport the next day, I saw that there were hourly flights to Havana full of Americans who did business with Cuba. Apparently, it was one of those things kept quiet, "out in the open." I felt a bit better. When we landed in Havana, we were surrounded by Cuban military. My fears dissipated as someone said, "Mr. Lamb, please come to the side." They took my banker's box full of books, handed each of us a *mojito* and took our passports. My brain was freaking! *They have my passport!*

We drove to our hotel escorted by military personnel, whom I later found out were also acting as bodyguards. Looking out the window, it felt like we were in a vintage photograph, circa 1958— as if time had stopped when Castro invaded Havana. That night at the hotel, after a meal and too many drinks, the interpreter grilled me. *He thinks I'm a spy,* I thought. So I went deep into my heart and said: "We teach people how to have success in business and access their spirits. I come in peace."

Up until that moment, it had not been decided whether Mr. Lamb's guests would participate in the meeting. But now, we were debriefed on how to conduct ourselves around Castro. Then someone told us that there would be soldiers above the ceiling in his office with machine guns at the ready. "If you move fast or look like you may harm El Comandante, they will kill you first and ask questions later." I was so scared, but I just kept telling myself, *Keep breathing. Trust in the Great Spirit. God would never send you here to die.*

The next day we arrived at Castro's awe-inspiring palace. I could barely hear my footsteps over the beating of my heart as we walked down a long marble hallway, surrounded by military men

---

*I was there on a mission much greater than me:
to do my first major job as a "peacemaker."*

---

with rifles. At the end of another long hallway, we were stopped, and a door to our left opened very discreetly. Since I was the last one to go in, I heard Castro before I saw him. "Señor Lamb, *muchas gracias,* I'm so happy you came."

Even though my brain was going a million miles an hour—*Don't look up, or they may kill you; what are you doing here?*—as I walked through the doorway and saw Castro shaking people's hands, I was filled with a centering energy, as though I had prepared for this moment my entire life.

Through the meeting, I was very appropriate. I only spoke when I was invited to do so. I was funny; I felt like a master of diplomacy. I was using skills that I didn't know I had. And when Castro, more handsome than his photos, finally turned to me to say, "You must be the Chilena," I was clear. I was truly living my calling. I was there on a mission much greater than me: to do my first major job as a "peacemaker."

We talked of the books I brought, and then I told him, "I am here to represent a whole group of Americans—" "Chilena, you are not American. You are from Chile," he interrupted. "I am a global citizen," I continued. "I am here to represent the world, and also a new 'world' of education, one that truly empowers people to become the geniuses they were born to be." I didn't know who was talking—I had never talked like that before!

"This group is so interesting. Cancel my next appointment, and bring more tea and snacks," Castro said, and soon we were engaged in the most amazing conversation. Later, after he had canceled several appointments to continue to speak with us, he said, "Chilena, I'm going to introduce you to my Minister of Education. Get a little group together and we will have a little party for you tonight."

When we we finally concluded that first meeting, I was the last one in line. I realized no one had instructed me how to say good-bye. *What do I do now?* All of a sudden, Castro put his arms around me and said, "Chilena, what a pleasure, the gifts you bring!" He gave me a hug, and as I reached to hug him back, I felt his beard, the beard of the famous dictator, the terrorist, the killer. *He's hugging me and his heart is open.*

Standing in the elevator, watching Castro wave goodbye to our little group, my own heart opened a thousand times. I started crying and said, "I believe my whole life just changed." Bill held my hand and said, "It did."

I had had the experience I intended to have. Now I knew I could trust that the metaphysical principles actually worked— that we do really create our experiences; that clearing our limiting thoughts is the key; that we are an instrument of the Divine; and that we are designed to make a difference to others, to make a contribution and to work on a daily basis to come as close as we can to fulfilling our life purpose.

Mr. Lamb died later that year. I never forgot him. A few years later, Bill Galt went back to Cuba. He shared that Castro asked, "How's the Chilena?" It's good to know that a little girl from Chile, who followed her heart as far as she could, was able to bring a little light to the consciousness of the world's longest-standing dictator. Though it took another six years for me to begin to work with other leaders and people of influence who support the acceleration of my mission, I may never have followed my life's purpose had I not faced my fears and embarked on one of the scariest (and most exciting) transformational experiences of my life.

Dame DC Cordova, CEO of Excellerated Business Schools®/Money & You®, is a pioneer in personal and professional development. Her purpose is to uplift the consciousness of humanity through business, and she works tirelessly to transform educational systems around the world so they may become active in the eradication of poverty and hunger. Connect with DC at www.DCCordova.com, or www.MoneyandYou.com.

Dr. Ray Charles

The Ray of Light

Tempers were running high in my Chicago firm. I'd even seen a colleague pick up a glass bottle during a scuffle with the CEO. A few days later, there was a mass exodus of employees, and shortly after they all left, the CEO came into my office. "Ray, follow me to the conference room." My heart raced, beating ten times for every step I took toward that room. I couldn't imagine what I'd done wrong.

In the conference room, on a long mahogany table, sat some papers and a pen. "Ray," the CEO said, "in order to continue your employment here, you need to be fully aligned with my practices and philosophy. Otherwise, you need to sign these termination papers."

My heart stopped, and my throat constricted. "May I have a moment to consider?" I asked the CEO. He nodded, and I left the room.

For some time, I'd been nagged by a calling—a deep desire to be a spiritual coach to leaders, helping them align their decisions, their lifestyles, and their businesses with truth, integrity and justice. The one person who knew the clarity of that calling was my best friend and most trusted advisor, my wife. But neither of us knew when it was time to respond to the call. I went to my office and phoned her to tell her about the CEO's ultimatum. "Babe," I said, "I believe this is it." To which she replied, "Come on home, hon."

I walked back into the conference room and signed the termination papers. And I stepped into my new life filled with the darkness of the unknown.

I'd entered this darkness before, as a child. When I was seven years old, my mom said to me one night, "Get dressed, I have a meeting with the owner of our new home." I quickly did as she asked. My nickname was "Tōn," and as we walked to the bus stop,

---

I walked back into the conference room and signed the termination papers. And I stepped into my new life filled with the darkness of the unknown. I'd entered this darkness before, as a child.

---

she turned to me and said, "Tōn, we're going to have our own home after tonight." We definitely needed one. For a year, my family— parents and six siblings—had been living with my grandmother in her small house.

After we disembarked from the bus that took us across town, my mother said, "Tōn, there's a short way and a long way to the owner of the house." She described the long way, a journey that would have taken an appreciable amount of time, so I said, "What's the short way, Mother?" "Through the cemetery," she replied. I grabbed her hand, took a deep breath, and said, "Let's go the short way."

Cemeteries in Trinidad are pretty nondescript—fields of green with no overt tombstones or ostentatious mausoleums, just row upon row of nearly identical headstones, rounded and meek. I remember distinctly the smell of death, of overripe decay, and the sound of myriad insects: crickets chirping at random distances and mosquitoes buzzing and whining in my ears. And I also recall the seamless and enveloping dark, a sky absent of moon and stars, an unending landscape minus any house light, street lamp or far-reaching beam of any passing car. I was terrified.

It was so dark I could not see my feet or my mother's face. *I'm walking over bodies*, I thought. Thousands of dead bodies surrounded us. The dirt beneath our feet was lumpy, and I wasn't sure if that was normal or because a new body was either going in or coming out! I grabbed her hand more tightly and asked, "Mother, are you scared?" "No," she said, quick but not brusque. "Are you?" she asked. "No," I said, but of course I was. When we exited the cemetery, I felt like all the weight of the world had been lifted from my shoulders.

We arrived at the owner's house, but no one was home. We sat on the front steps and waited for over an hour before the owner arrived. Mrs. Mamet was a pudgy woman, middle-aged, her face creased by toil, and she wore a less-than-fresh flower print dress. My mother met her and said, "We heard one of your houses was available, and we're here because we'd like to take it."

Mrs. Mamet shook her head and said, "I'm sorry, that house has already been promised to someone else."

My mother's entire spirit sank. Her shoulders dropped, her eyes looked downcast, and I thought she was about to fall onto the steps. But then she raised her being and said, out of nowhere,

---

Her eyes held a gentle yet unbending resolve that was impossible to ignore.

"I know that you've already promised that house to another, but I firmly believe that house belongs to me and my family." Her eyes held a gentle yet unbending resolve that was impossible to ignore.

"Well," Mrs. Mamet said, "you walked through the pitch-dark cemetery, and you waited at my home for over an hour, so I'll refer you to the landlord of the house. I know it's already been awarded to someone else, but if you firmly believe this is your home, then Miss Parker is the woman you need to visit." It was almost ten o'clock. To get to the landlord's house we had to walk back through the cemetery. Back through the complete darkness and over the bodies. This time I wasn't frightened. I had triumphed over all of my fears because I now shared my mother's conviction. I was amazed that I was not frightened; I felt like a superhero.

We arrived at the landlord's house, and it was completely dark. We didn't know if they were out for the night or asleep, so Mother knocked loudly, and there was no answer. She knocked again, louder, more insistently, and again there was no answer. It wasn't until the third set of knocks that we got a response. A light from within came on, a window was raised, and a head poked out into the night.

"Who are you?" said Miss Parker, a woman slightly older than Mrs. Mamet. "Do you have any idea how late it is?"

My mother's plea came out in a torrent: "Hello, my name is Mrs. Charles, and I just left Mrs. Mamet's house, and she told me that this house across the street has already been awarded to someone, but I truly *believe* this house is mine and belongs to my family." My mother paused, perhaps to catch her breath, and in that pause came no response. So my mother, out of nowhere, blurted out, "I'm the daughter of Eugenia Millington."

"Eugenia Millington?" Miss Parker said, surprised. "The cook at our area hospital? She's your mother?" "Yes," my mother replied, "she is my mother." "Wait a minute," Miss Parker said. She pulled her head out of the window and disappeared for a few moments before she returned, this time through the door. She handed my mother a key. "Eugenia is a beautiful woman," she said. "I promised that house to someone else, but that is now my problem. In honor of your mother, I'm giving you that house, and here is the key."

That moment was the birthing place of my call to the ministry. The call would not come to fruition until years later, but that was the moment I learned of the irrepressible power of a single ray of light. The image of light in the darkness became crucial to me after I left my job in Chicago. I was walking into the unknown and possibly sacrificing my dream home, my family's stability, my financial endowment, my net worth, everything. But I was convinced my call was real, and I'd heard somewhere before that "conviction is not conviction unless it's going to cost you something."

A week after I left the Chicago firm, my wife hosted a huge exodus party. It was catered and had over one hundred of my closest friends, as though my wife had already had it all lined up and was simply waiting for me to follow through on my call. Still, I felt guilty and ashamed at no longer being able to provide for my family, and though my friends were wishing me well, I could tell that they were wondering if I was nuts.

Deep down, I agreed with them, condemning my own actions. I would say to myself, "What makes you think you are qualified for this call? You have no experience in coaching, you have no one to model after. And why now? Why not after you've established a sizable nest egg and your family is well provided for?"

However, in the ensuing days, the thought kept coming back to me, "What if I call and ask if I could get a discount if I only attend the final workshop and not the entire convention?"

The months that followed were a dark season. I appreciated the love and support I received from my spouse and spiritual coaching clients, but the thought of being a failure was such a regular visitor, it assumed its own real estate in my mind, reminding me continually of the saying in my faith that *"if any provide not for his own, and specially for those of his own house, he has denied the faith, and is worse than an infidel."*

Two years into my journey, I came across an ad in a business journal that read, "How to grow spiritually while growing a multi-million-dollar business." The ad highlighted the final workshop of a week-long venture capital convention in Dallas, Texas. "It would be great to attend this convention, just to hear the speaker at this final workshop," I thought, but then discarded the idea because of the price tag of the convention.

However, in the ensuing days, the thought kept coming back to me, "What if I call and ask if I could get a discount if I only attend the final workshop and not the entire convention?" Several days later, I finally placed the call. Once connected, I announced my name and my interest in attending the final workshop. The person on the line kept saying, "Wait a minute, *the* Dr. Ray Charles? The spiritual coach?" I responded, "Yes, I am Dr. Ray Charles, and yes, I am a spiritual coach." The gentleman then said, "Sir, we have been trying to get in contact with you for months. You were referred to us, but we misplaced your contact information. If you look at the ad, you will notice it says, 'mystery speaker.'"

I looked at the ad and sure enough, it read "mystery speaker." The gentleman then said, "Sir, the mystery speaker at this conference is you. We were running out of time in going to print so we decided to post the ad, believing and trusting that some way, somehow, we would get in contact with you." In that very moment, my feelings of fear, guilt, shame and loss were suddenly shattered.

Like my mother, I have held onto my conviction, not knowing fully "how" the call will manifest. Have there been hiccups along the way, have there been hurts and disappointments? Absolutely, but the lesson I learned at age seven is the guiding light for me: *In the face of adversity, stay true to what you believe.* Through the darkness of the cemetery, Mother held on to what she believed. And just as my grandmother Eugenia Millington gave my mother a ray of light, my mother's conviction became this little Tōn's ray of light. I continue to hold onto what I believe, fully ready to pay the price for my conviction.

Dr. Charles holds bachelor's and master's degrees in chemical engineering from Howard University and a doctorate in biblical counseling from North Carolina College of Theology. He is an executive coach, author and spiritual mentor to a plethora of leaders, including CEOs, pastors, political leaders, stay-at-home moms and college students. His mission is "To be a Ray of Light® to leaders to position them to hold true to what they believe, no matter what." Connect with Dr. Charles at www.DrRayCharles.com.

Susie Carder

The Right Mother

It's eighteen years ago now, but I'll never forget the day my daughter Amanda stepped bawling off the bus from kindergarten, her face streaming bewildered tears. I ran to her, swept her up in my arms and stroked her curly hair. "Baby, what's wrong?" She was sobbing so hard she could barely hiccup the answer: "Mom—my teacher said I was evil."

"What?" I gasped. "What do you *mean* she said you're evil?" "She said black represents evil," Amanda replied. "And white represents purity." With a mixture of outrage and grief, I looked at my beautiful little girl, at her caramel-colored skin, her full lips, her big brown eyes brimming with hurt, and realized: she's different. I had felt different as a little girl, too, with no mother at home to raise me like it seemed everyone else had. But that difference could remain a secret from most of the rest of the world, unlike the obvious difference in the color of my daughters' skin.

Infuriated, I drove right down to the school to confront Amanda's teacher. "Oh my goodness, I'm so sorry," she apologized. "I had no idea. No child has ever made that connection before." "You had no idea? How irresponsible!" I did not try to hide my anger. "We were just discussing concepts," she faltered. "But you're looking at a little African-American child," I said. "Don't you understand what that might mean to her?" The teacher was remorseful, but I was appalled at her ignorance. She didn't even know that she didn't know.

I looked around the school with new eyes—the eyes of a mother of black children. There were no other black children there. There were no teachers of color, no leaders of color in the school—just the reality I had plunked my kids into.... a white world. I was ashamed at my own ignorance and unconscious actions. I wasn't any better than the oblivious teacher.

Amanda was different. And so was her little sister, my daughter Megan: two African-American children with a white mother. Because I am white and didn't know what it was to be black, because I didn't *see* color, because they were my children and I simply loved them, because Amanda went to a Christian

---

I was ashamed at my own ignorance and unconscious actions. I wasn't any better than the oblivious teacher.

---

school where they preached love and inclusivity, because our (predominantly white) community supposedly accepted everyone regardless of color, I hadn't understood until this day what being black could mean for my babies.

I recalled the dirty looks and name-calling their father and I had experienced while we were dating and later when we got married: White men called me "n*%*er-lover;" black women sneered at me and told me to quit stealing all the good black men.

I was so hurt and disgusted by this ignorance and shallowness. I chose my husband because I loved him. He made me feel special. It didn't matter to me what color he was—I saw love, a future and a family with him. My father, now a loving grandfather to his adored granddaughters, was once a racist who disowned me when I married my husband: "If you marry him," he stormed, "you'll never set foot in this house again." The hatred and ignorance came from all sides.

Before I got married, a client of mine told me, "I want you to think long and hard about this." I thought she just meant marriage. "What about those children?" she continued. *What do you mean, what about those children? My God, how rude!* I thought. "They're going to be judged and harassed." *No, they're not! I'm going to love them, and be the best mother I can be to them.*

"Baby," I said, meeting Megan's big brown eyes in the mirror, "Why do you want to be like me?"
"Because I want to be white and pretty like you," she said.

And love will conquer all… how naïve! Now I finally understood the context for what she had told me. I had suddenly awakened to some perception of reality for people of color, and my eyes would never close again. It was about my children, now.

Young, confused and a bit scared, I thought, *My children need help to grow up with a strong sense of self in a society that teaches children black is evil and white is good. How will I teach them to love themselves when I can never fully understand or share their experience?* Feeling powerless in one moment and powerful in the next, I knew I had to create an environment for my kids where they could learn a healthy sense of self-esteem, a sense of self. First, I moved out of a great community and got my girls into a diverse school.

The integrated school and community were a step, but not enough to counteract the messages of a whole society. The melting pot of kids who came over never wanted to play with Pocahontas, or the brown baby dolls—they wanted Barbie. She was "the prettiest." My heart ached—this was worse than I had imagined. One day, when Megan was six, I was driving with her in the backseat. I had tossed a pair of white pantyhose back there. "Look, Mommy!" she cried in excitement. "I'm like you, now!" I looked in the rearview mirror and saw that she had pulled the white pantyhose out of their package and onto both her little brown arms. "Baby," I said, meeting Megan's big brown eyes in the mirror, "Why do you want to be like me?"

"Because I want to be white and pretty like you," she said.

Good grief! I thought. *She'll never be white like me, nor should she want to. And if she's always trying to be something she's not, she'll have a miserable life.* It broke my heart that she thought she had to be white to be considered worthy or pretty. How wrong! *I created this—I've got to figure out a way for her to be happy in her own beautiful caramel skin, with being a proud, powerful black woman.* As a white woman with limited access to the African-American community where I was never really accepted, I had my work cut out for me. But I was willing to swallow my pride and push past my fears—anything for my daughters.

The girls' dad primarily dated white women. My second husband was white. Most of my friends were white. I didn't want my daughters to see only a white world; they needed to see themselves. I had to find a role model for them who represented

---

She educated me once again, saying, "That's who I am here, Mom. When people look at me, they don't see mixed or white. They only see black." I realized that I was still learning.

---

strength, femininity, peace, love and being okay with being *black*. It became my quest to create a community filled with powerful women of all colors, sizes and shapes, so the girls could decide exactly who they wanted to be—but I knew I needed HELP. Then I listened to a powerful speaker—an African-American woman named Lisa Nichols—share a poem celebrating her unique beauty.

In a soft, yet assured, rhythmic voice, she said: "I have learned to love my round hips, full lips, mocha skin and my kinky hair. I no longer apologize for my existence; I embrace it, I love me exactly as I am." Before I knew it, I was crying. *This is what I want for my girls.* My heart leapt with hope. After the event, I took a huge leap of faith. Willing to be unreasonably bold for my children, I approached Lisa Nichols and asked her to become a mentor to my daughters. Though she was kind and respectful, I could tell she was surprised by my request. My heart beating fast, I opened up even more than I expected. "I have no choice," I said.

Lisa listened as I told the story of our family. I said, "I can be a loving mom, I can be a GREAT mom, but at the end of the day I am a white woman raising black children. And as much as I don't want to admit it, I need someone who can show them how to be proud African-American women in a world that is prejudiced, unfair and sometimes cruel."

I could see Lisa trying to comprehend what it felt like for me to have to say those words. Then she looked me in the eyes and said, "Susie, I would be honored to be in Amanda and Megan's lives." For over ten years now, I have been reminded daily that it was the right decision.

Even with their amazing mentors and role models, my daughters have had challenges learning to love and embrace themselves in a culture that celebrates the "white is better than the rest" myth, a culture that tells them they are not worthy, smart or beautiful because they are African-American.

In one of the most devastating periods of my life, I almost lost Megan to this myth, as she starved herself to look like white girls on TV and tried to mute the voice of her self-doubt with drugs. My child's life threatened, I hocked my house immediately to put her in treatment. *God, please save my child!* I prayed, as I did all I could. After eighteen months of battles, counseling and crying, our prayers were answered: when Megan made it out alive, she was finally her own woman.

More blessings flowed when Amanda was accepted at Harvard and got involved with black women's empowerment groups. Overjoyed, I made a comment about her getting in touch with her black culture. She educated me once again, saying, "That's who I am here, Mom. When people look at me, they don't see mixed or white. They only see black." I realized that I was still learning.

For all they have been through, my daughters have grown up to be amazing, self-assured women who act with compassion in service to their community. They are both natural leaders who can move a hushed room to weeping with the strength of their presence and their hearts. Megan, even without those damn white pantyhose, is a mini-me, with a fire in her belly that now refuses to be extinguished.

As parents, we want to be everything to and for our kids. At first, it hurt to realize I couldn't give them everything they needed, because underneath the important conversation of black and white was also my just needing to know—*am I good enough? Can I be the right mother to my babies?* My own mother left when I was five. If my own mother left me, how good could I really be?

But my challenge was a huge gift. I knew from not having a mom what I wanted to *be* as a mom. I could *create* "Mom." My lesson's unique twist was in learning how to transcend color, be aware of color and honor two women of color called "my girls."

Loving them, playing with them, being there for them, protecting them—I constantly asked myself, *am I doing it right? Am I saying the right things? Am I trying too hard?* Some of these questions are unanswerable. But when I witness Amanda and Megan living their lives full out, speaking, shining in their compassion, celebrating their caramel skin, full lips and round hips as strong, beautiful African-American women, I thank God we have triumphed. I am amazed they are mine. And I begin to see the inkling of an answer.

Susie Carder, COO/President of Motivating the Masses, is also a speaker and human highlighter who delivers keynote addresses, workshops and consulting projects for clients around the world and is the award-winning author of fifteen books and audio programs focusing on results-based sales systems and profit solutions. She has been a successful entrepreneur for over twenty years, having built and sold multiple businesses, including a software business that provides business tools and support to small independent business owners in the professional beauty industry. She was President of Salon Training International and helped build it into the number one training and consulting company in its industry before selling it to Thompson Learning. In 2006 she was named Dell's Top Technology Company of the Year, and in 2007 she won the Women Who Mean Business Award. In 2010 Susie was nominated for San Diego's Women Who Move the City Award. Connect with Susie at www.SusieCarder.com.

Lori J. Boehm

The Road Less Traveled

Tears silently ran down our faces as my husband and I listened to our priest administer last rites to our newborn son. It was the first time I saw my husband cry. Twenty-four hours earlier, this little soul had entered the world three months early, with lungs that had not grown enough to even allow him to breathe. At only two pounds, fifteen ounces, his body was not developed enough to sustain life. He had already had a brain seizure. Tubes came out of him everywhere. The doctors said that the first forty-eight hours would be critical and that "arrangements" needed to be made, for they did not think he was going to live and they did not want to give us any false hope.

Forty-eight hours later, I sat in my hospital ward with the other mothers. Each had given birth to a healthy, wonderful baby. Each of their rooms was full of well-wishers, cheerful cards and flowers. Each had been delivered long-stemmed red roses honoring the blessings of motherhood. Conversely, I had nothing. No calls, no visitors, no flowers or cards—and certainly no long-stemmed red roses. Because my son had been born so prematurely and was not expected to live, no one knew what to do.

My mother was out of state, other family members scattered. My husband was stoic, unwilling to discuss the complicated medical terms the doctors threw at us and unable to describe his feelings or help me sort out mine. I had no one to talk to. I couldn't even hold my son, touch him, comfort him. I felt so alone.

On the third day, I awoke in the middle of the night, consumed by the fear that my son would die. I knew I had to let go. I humbled myself before God and said, "Thy will be done." If my little son was to live, then it was up to God. If he didn't, then I trusted the Lord knew what was best for my precious baby. Two months later, I took Nicholas home. God had made his decision.

My son had three cousins, all similar in age. Those cousins crawled around the tree, ran around the table, laughed and talked like kids on Christmas are supposed to. But not Nicholas. He hardly moved.

For the next year, I played with him, snuggled with him, cuddled with him and thanked God every day that Nicholas had lived and been returned to us.

Deep down, I could tell something was wrong with him, but I wouldn't let that knowledge surface. I lived in denial, but I was forced to face facts when we celebrated Nicholas' first Christmas with extended family. My son had three cousins, all similar in age. Those cousins crawled around the tree, ran around the table, laughed and talked like kids on Christmas are supposed to. But not Nicholas. He hardly moved.

After the holidays, I contacted Stanford Medical Center, where he had been born. They referred me to a medical clinic that specialized in childhood diseases. The physical therapist held Nicholas up and said, "See how his legs and feet are pointing down?" "Yes," I replied. "That's not normal," she continued. Then, she gave me the diagnosis. "Nicholas has spastic quadriplegic cerebral palsy. He will not be able to walk, talk, or feed himself." Finally, I knew the truth and it was brutal. Seeing the shock and sadness on my face, the physical therapist said, "Lori, you should institutionalize him."

With tears running down my face, I drove toward my mother's house. I was devastated. Why hadn't I seen this before? Then I became very angry. Why hadn't our pediatrician noticed? And if he had, why didn't he say anything to me? When I confronted our long-time family doctor, he said, "I suspected Nicholas had cerebral palsy. I just didn't have the heart to tell you."

I was at a fork in the road of life: one road was to institutionalize my sweet baby; the other was to defy all odds and raise him myself. I made my decision. *I will not institutionalize my son,* I resolved. *No matter what I have to do, his life will be the most normal life possible.* From that day forward, Nicholas' life was as normal as I could make it. On Halloweens I dressed him as a clown, an Ewok and other popular characters. He loved to bowl, played T-ball and

> *It appeared as though my son was the only one in the room who could pay attention, follow directions, read and do some basic math. I was appalled.*

tennis, went horseback riding and attended summer camp. He did well in school from first through third grade in spite of being in a segregated school where only disabled children were enrolled. This was a credit to his wonderful teachers.

On the first day of fourth grade, I got him to his classroom. The desks were in neat rows, the walls were a bright, happy yellow, and all seemed fine. At first. I then realized that half the children from last year, as well as the teacher, were gone. And the new children were more severely disabled. It appeared as though my son was the only one in the room who could pay attention, follow directions, read and do some basic math. I was appalled.

When a disabled child enters school, the school district and the parents enter into a contract called an Individualized Education Program (IEP). This throws parents of disabled children into a world that has its own language. Under the letter of the law, special needs children are required to be educated in the Least Restrictive

Environment, or LRE. This means that they are to be educated and socialized with their peers.

I walked away from the classroom shaking with anger. I demanded an IEP meeting with the school principal and appropriate school staff, as was my right. At the meeting, I stated, "I don't want him in that classroom. It cannot provide him the growth opportunity that he deserves. It will simply be a babysitting class!" "That classroom is where he belongs," the Director of Special Education said dismissively, "We're not moving him." *Lady,* I thought, *you've just set yourself up for the fight of your life.*

I'd learned from my dad, an attorney, that there was a law book on every subject—I just had to go and find it. After a great deal of study about what my son was legally entitled to educationally, I armed myself with as much knowledge as possible and headed

---

The teacher paused for a long time, thinking. She stared into my eyes, as if trying to figure out if I could be trusted. Finally, Ms. Sturgis gritted her teeth, exhaled loudly and said, "Let's get your son educated."

---

into battle. All semester, I fought with my son's school. Just before Christmas, at yet another IEP meeting, the Director of Special Education pulled me aside. "We are not buckling," she said in an angry, sneering manner. "I will fight you as long as it takes and as much as it takes. You WILL take my offer!" Afraid for Nicholas' academic future, I did take her offer—a classroom filled to capacity, with just one teacher and no aide. I thought it was the best I could get.

One day after school, I visited my son's new teacher, Ms. Sturgis. I wondered if she knew what the school district was up to. After visiting with her, I took a leap of faith and said, "The school has set you and my son up for failure. The Director is using you to prove that Nicholas is not capable of being out of a segregated, low-functioning special needs class. I don't want him to fail, but

I can't do it without your help." The teacher paused for a long time, thinking. She stared into my eyes, as if trying to figure out if I could be trusted. Finally, Ms. Sturgis gritted her teeth, exhaled loudly and said, "Let's get your son educated."

Nicholas and Ms. Sturgis spent many days together after school. She gave him extra time and instruction in all of his academic areas. Under the tutelage of this wonderful teacher, Nicholas gained phenomenal study habits and a hunger for knowledge. Eventually, with the help of great teachers and a very determined, tenacious warrior mom, Nicholas finished high school with a 3.0 point G.P.A. and was college bound.

Watching Nicholas graduate from high school, I thought, *I'm done! No more IEPs! No more fighting with the school system!* A feeling of relief washed over me. I had done my job. We had beaten the system. Most kids with cerebral palsy don't graduate; they get a certificate. Yet here was Nicholas, receiving his diploma just like all of the other seniors.

The system didn't have to live with its decisions day in and day out, but we did. Therefore I had decided I would become the most determined, knowledgeable, powerful and skilled advocate for Nicholas that I could possibly be. Nicholas helped me find my passion; the system made a warrior of me! Over the years, I'd learned too much just to discard clues to my path. Surely God wanted something more of me, but what?

In an instant, the answer came: Become an advocate for other children. For ten years, I have been a successful special needs advocate for many children and their families, and a lobbyist for the disabled. I believe strongly, and continue to believe, that lawmakers MUST hear the voices of the disabled before they make decisions that affect them.

The first time I testified before the California State Senate, I took a moment to remember the nights I feared Nicholas would die, and the day I decided I would take the road less traveled and dedicate my life to ensuring *his* life was as normal as possible. I realized that, without Nicholas and all he inspired, I would not have my passion, and hundreds of disabled children might never have all that they are entitled to under the law. Standing before the Senate, I thought, *God truly did have a plan for Nicholas and for me. Onward!*

Lori J. Boehm received her BS in child development/special education. She is certified in The Special Education Advocacy Training (SEAT) Project, has served as a board member of the Ventura County Autism Society and acts as Disabilities Consultant for State Senator Tony Strickland. In 2010, in honor of her years of successful advocacy and her influence over legislation affecting children with special needs, Lori was named Woman of the Year in her state Senate district. Connect with Lori at www. AdvocateForSpecialNeeds.com.

John D. McQueen

Getting in Position

Sitting across the dinner table, my daughter was ecstatic as she told my wife and I about her final day at camp. I tried to smile, but it was impossible. After she finished, I said, "Baby, Daddy's got some bad news." The room got solemn; I hated to be the bearer of such bad news. "We cannot send you back to your school."

Her eyes went wide in disbelief. "Why, Daddy?" she asked. "We just don't have the money, sweetheart. I'm sorry." She started crying, wailing in such a painful way that I couldn't stand it. I went to the bathroom, sat on the toilet and began to cry. I buried my head in my hands, wanting to smother my own wailing to protect my family from the depth of my own pain.

How did it come to this? I thought. *When did my well-planned life change for the worse?* Two years earlier, I'd been promoted by General Electric's NBC-TV and moved my family to Atlanta. But then I was axed during a downsizing. Since then my financial life had barreled toward ruin like a race car with no brakes headed toward a cliff! We had a brand-new baby, and a huge new house we could no longer afford. And now we had to remove my elder daughter from the private Christian school she loved. *Haven't I been through enough? Haven't I paid my dues?* As I sat in the bathroom, my mind wandered back to a different dinner table, many years ago...

We were upstairs in Junie's room playing electric football. We lived and breathed sports so much that we'd play outside as late into the autumn as we could, but this was mid-December in North Philly, with ten inches of snow on the ground, and no one was playing anything outside. Junie's real name was June, June Bellamy. I was in second grade, he was in third, and we were best friends. It was red team vs. blue team. We used the "Big Sneaker" for kicking field goals, making the little magnetic football bounce around the vibrating table. It was getting late, getting dark, and I knew exactly what time it was in Junie's house.

> That's why I often positioned myself to be
> at a friend's house at suppertime. I rotated
> among various friends so as not to wear out my
> welcome at any one house, and sometimes I'd
> decline one offer to assure more in the future.

I didn't know what his mom was cooking, but I could smell it all the way upstairs, and I was hungry. "Boys, time for dinner," his dad yelled. Junie and I went into the hallway. His teenaged brother, Mike, was there. "I had a hunch you'd still be here, Half-head," he said, playfully poking my chest. I walked in front of him to the kitchen, and he kept playfully slapping my shoulder. I didn't mind that he knew what I was up to. I was used to being the joke of the neighborhood, the kid everyone picked on. I was awkward, taller than most boys my age, pathetically skinny and very seldom had nice clothes or wore the latest styles. With my oddly-shaped head, I was an easy target. Some days it seemed the whole world enjoyed making fun of me, but eventually I began to use the teasing and ridicule to my benefit: it became my motivation to get out of my neighborhood and find a better life.

"John," Mrs. Bellamy said, "Would you like to join us for dinner?" The table was already set for eight, and there were only seven Bellamys; I noticed that the minute I stepped into the kitchen. On the table sat a huge pot roast, green beans, mashed potatoes and warm rolls. I looked to Mr. Bellamy, and he nodded his approval of the invitation. "I'd appreciate that, Mrs. Bellamy," I said. "I bet you would, mooch," Mike said, and his two sisters giggled. *Still, I stayed. I stayed because I was determined to get one good meal that day.*

My mother, Dellar Mae McQueen, was an aspiring singer who hooked up with local bands for gigs in the tri-state area. I have no idea who my father was. Mom was also into alcohol and drugs and had other mental health issues, so I often took care of myself. We lived in a two-room apartment with few amenities. Our landlady, Mrs. Baines, lived downstairs. I called her Aunt Baines, but she wasn't. She helped look after me, fixed me dinner and bought me groceries, but she couldn't do that all the time. That's why I often positioned myself to be at a friend's house at suppertime. I rotated

---

Even as a child, I knew that most of the factors that made my childhood difficult were not my fault. But I also knew that I couldn't use those factors as excuses not to do what needed to be done.

---

among various friends so as not to wear out my welcome at any one house, and sometimes I'd decline one offer to assure more in the future.

When I was ten, my mom had another baby, my little brother. But when I was twelve, Mom had to be institutionalized, so I was put in foster care. Over the next four years, I lived in three different foster homes, but mostly I lived in the home of Ms. Zulaykha Salah. She was a severe Black Muslim woman who provided a clean, safe environment and three good meals per day, but very little nurturing and love.

When I was thirteen, city transportation workers went on strike for forty-four days. Even though I lived in North Philly with Ms. Salah, I still went to school in West Philly, five miles away, and depended upon public transportation. "Ms. Salah," I said just after the strike had begun, "could you drive me to school in the morning?" She had a real nice car, a red Cougar, with a white vinyl top. She was retired, so she had plenty of time, and I thought she'd want to help me get my education. "No," she said, curtly.

I had no idea why she wouldn't drive me to school. It didn't matter, I was going to school; I would get out of that neighborhood. I'd already seen too many kids in my neighborhood stabbed, shot, selling drugs or winding up in prison before they were even twenty-one. My life may have been hard, but prison was harder, and prison was riddled with people who didn't graduate. I had to get to school by any means necessary.

Even as a child, I knew that most of the factors that made my childhood difficult were not my fault. But I also knew that I couldn't use those factors as excuses not to do what needed to be done.

The next morning, I woke up early enough to walk to school—out of the house at 6:45. I wore my basketball shoes, and as I walked I wondered about a lot of things—would I be late, what would my first car be, what was next in my life. At Parkside Avenue, I got hyper-alert: tough neighborhood. Plenty of kids were beaten and shot there; there was no reason I couldn't be another. *So I walked.*

The strike went on for weeks. I wore holes in my shoes, so I put cardboard in them, but the cardboard lasted only a couple of days. I started walking to school in my dress shoes. It was uncomfortable walking, and I got blisters, so each morning I had to bandage and tape my heels before setting out. But those shoes had thick soles, and I knew they would last the duration of the strike. They did.

When I was fourteen, the state deemed my mother fit to take care of us again. My foster care caseworker called me to his office one afternoon after school. It was a small, ugly room with dingy yellow walls, a dull metal desk, and half a dozen tall file cabinets. "I have some good news for you, John," he said to me with a smile—as if he understood my life, which he probably did. "You can go back to living with your mother!" I was always confronted with tough choices—school or the streets, basketball or drugs, Mom or Ms. Salah. But I was able to think long term, and my goal was to get out of my neighborhood.

In my head I screamed, *my mother still wants me!* But that excitement was quickly replaced by anxiety. I had to make a choice: Go back and live with my mother, whom I loved deeply but knew couldn't take care of me, or go live with Mrs. Salah, who was mean, strict and angry but could provide a safe place and three meals a

---

My whole life had been about getting myself in position. It had never guaranteed that I got dinner, but it did guarantee that a seat at the table, any table, was possible.

---

day? I thought about it for what seemed to be an eternity, but was only a few seconds. The caseworker said, "John, did you hear me?" I blurted out, "I want to stay with Ms. Salah." Yes. That's right. The love I felt for my mother was so real. But so was my fear of being stuck forever in the suffering that had become so normal for so many people. I had to get out, and Mrs. Salah was the way for me to do it.

I graduated from high school and Cabrini College. I entered the corporate arena. My skill level wasn't higher than anyone else's, but I was determined no one would outwork me. I figured if I just kept showing up and had a good attitude, I could prosper. And I did. I moved all the way up to Director of Business Development for all NBC-TV-owned and operated stations in the Southeast Region. That's why we moved to Atlanta.

And now I was headed over a cliff. I left the bathroom and went to my daughter's bedroom. She slept so peacefully it was impossible to tell that, hours before, I'd shattered her life by telling her I had to take her out of her school. The longer I stood there, the more resolved I became to not let this happen. Our public schools in Georgia ranked forty-eighth out of fifty. How could I subject my daughter to that?

I thought about Junie's dinner table, and how I'd strategized getting a hot meal. My whole life had been about getting myself in position. It had never guaranteed that I got dinner, but it did guarantee that a seat at the table, any table, was possible. I needed to get myself in position again, and fast. A few days later, my wife came to me with a new business venture. I could see the hope and possibility in her eyes when she asked, "What do you think?" I looked it over and knew why she was excited. "We are going to move heaven and earth to make this work," I blurted. And we did—each of us working a full-time job, each of us taking care of our kids, each of us using any moment of spare time to help move our new venture forward.

One year later, our family was at dinner again, and my daughter was telling another fascinating story. After she finished, I said, "Daddy's got some news to tell you." Her face had a frightened look. "No, baby, it's different this time." She looked scared but trusting. I softly said, "I want you in the best position for your future, so I want you to go to the best college you can." She nodded. "In order to do that, you need to go to the best schools you can." There was a small pause. I could tell that she was holding her breath, waiting for the bomb to drop. "That's why, tomorrow, we'll enroll you in another private Christian school."

After a moment or two passed and the information sank in, joy erupted like a volcano, complete with jumping up and down, screaming cheers of celebration and one of the best hugs a daddy could ever experience. And in that moment, I could see why I chose to sit at Junie's dinner table; why I chose to walk holes into my shoes to get to school; and why I chose to live with Ms. Salah over my mother. I was willing to do whatever it took to get into position to let my own light shine, and position my family to do the same.

John D. McQueen, entrepreneur, business coach and transformational speaker, is committed to helping everyday people find their very own greatness and live the fulfilled life he and his family have come to know. John has entrepreneurial interests in several industries, including health and wellness, goods distribution and entertainment. Connect with John at www.JMcQueenIsLivingProof.com.

Michiyo Ambrosius, PhD

The Color of Freedom

A newspaper article I read as a teenager in Japan one day changed my whole life. It described a dead farm-girl just a few years older than me. She had been found with her eyes closed, face contorted in pain, clutching a pair of red high-heeled shoes—an apparent case of suicide.

I was born into a middle-class family on the outskirts of Tokyo. When I became a teenager in the 1960s, Japanese society was still very closed and traditional, and so were women's prescribed roles. Girls were expected to be nice, quiet, submissive and obedient, holding our hands in front of our mouths when we laughed and deferring to every authority but our own inner voice. We were puppets—silenced, wrapped, boxed in, convenient tools of society. Silent voices said, "BE LIKE THIS—" pointing to the white-masked face of a geisha, her eyes downcast, her perfect rosebud lips perpetually painted closed.

All of our behaviors were closely monitored for propriety. We had to talk and behave and dress only in certain ways. Arranged marriages were still the cultural norm, so we could expect to be married off to men we didn't even know. We could then look forward to our ultimate fulfillment: spending the rest of our lives caring for our husband's parents, our husbands, our children and our immaculately clean homes. This was not what I had in mind for my own future. It sounded like a kind of death.

I loved the movie, *Rebel Without A Cause*. I identified with the alienated teenagers whose parents were absent, out-of-touch or even abusive, like my own tyrannical mother, who terrified everyone in the family. I tried so hard to make her happy, but it didn't matter how well I behaved. Sometimes she would throw me from one corner of a room to another, or hit me until my grandmother begged her to stop. My father said nothing.

So when I opened the paper that day and read the article about the farm-girl from outside Tokyo who had taken rat poison—a horrible, painful death—at eighteen, and was found with her arms wrapped around those beautiful red shoes, I knew instantly why

> *This was not what I had in mind for my own future. It sounded like a kind of death.*

she had killed herself. She saw no future. The red shoes she carried to her death sent a loud message for a girl silenced in a traditional life. I saw them as a symbol of the life she'd never have: one of freedom, fulfillment, choice, self-discovery and self-expression. My stomach hit the floor. *I have to leave.*

I had already overheard my parents talking about their plans for my future. After I graduated, they might send me to a two-year junior college. Maybe. Then they would marry me off. *Wait a minute!* I thought. *No way!* Every cell of my body rebelled against being railroaded into an arranged marriage, but it wasn't until I read the article that I knew I had to escape my own version of the farm-girl's fate. I was fifteen.

If I stayed, I thought, my heart, my dreams and my soul would be shattered, like hers. I kept my plans secret from my parents, and for the next five years I worked to save enough money for my passage to the United States by cargo boat, the cheapest alternative in those days when women wore white gloves and pillbox hats, and airplanes were horrendously expensive. I worked as a bookstore clerk and tutored a wealthy medical doctor's three small children. I knew I was lucky just to be able to work outside the home, and I was so independent, so resistant to my mother's attempts to control me that I didn't even ask my parents for spending money.

Someone later told me, "You can endure anything if you know it will end sometime soon." That was how I felt about life in Tokyo in the years before I left. Every time I despaired or got frustrated with the slow process of my journey toward freedom, I said to myself, *This is temporary.* Sometimes, I felt horrifyingly humiliated by my

---

If I stayed, I thought, my heart, my dreams and my soul would be shattered, like hers.

---

mother's rage-a-holic tirades, and even got to the point of thinking, *Either I kill myself or her.* What terrified me the most was my own rage. What if I burst out of my own skin? But often, I surprised myself with my own strength and stamina. I had never known my will to live and grow were so strong.

After graduating high school, I entered junior college, as my parents had planned, and continued working and saving for my boat passage. I had learned just enough English by now to draft a letter to the editors of a number of small newspapers in the United States with the aid of my Japanese-English dictionary. It took days. And it was a very humbling experience. I was worried my letter would not be good enough. But I posted it anyway.

"Dear Editor," I wrote, nervous that my English was too awkward, that they would all just laugh at me and throw my letter away— "My name is Michiyo, and I am a female student in Japan. I would like to experience life in the United States and attend school there. I am completing junior college in Tokyo now, but am willing to attend a high school in the United States as an auditing student to improve my English until I am ready to progress to college study. I am looking for a family that would like to host me and provide shelter for me when I arrive, and exchange cultural knowledge. I thank you for your help in printing this letter in your newspaper."

When an editor in a small town in Indiana put my letter in his paper, and a kind, elderly couple responded to it, I was elated and a little surprised. I started saving even more money for a Greyhound bus ticket from Los Angeles to Indiana.

My parents were very surprised to hear my news about a month before my departure, but they could not object to my plans. For them, too, the United States was a land of dreams and gold, success and freedom. Since I planned to pay for my own education in the United States, they could not argue with me or try to control me with money. I would not have listened if they had. I could no longer tolerate my mother's violence or an authority outside my inner knowing—something inside me would no longer allow it. Everything was in place, I had the tickets in hand that I'd worked five whole years to buy, and by then I couldn't wait to leave Japan. I felt strengthened by my swelling anger. My heart burned with hope, and the spirit of adventure. It was 1965.

My parents saw me off the morning I left Japan. As the boat pulled away from the harbor and I stared at the shore, my whole life so far receding and getting smaller, I cried. Suddenly, I felt fearful and uncertain. My home had been abusive, but at least I knew it was home. That was less frightening than the unknown. I had been so busy working for freedom, propelled by the image of the farm-girl and her futile life, I hadn't thought I'd feel lonely and scared as well as thrilled and liberated.

The voyage was exciting. There were only ten passengers on the cargo boat, and I made friends with three other young women travelers. We ate our meals with the captain of the ship, who delighted us with bizarre and funny stories of his travels, the many strange and beautiful places he had seen. As I listened to his recollections, I felt my own courage rise. I wondered what California, or New York City, would be like.

On the tenth day, we sailed into San Francisco, all of us cheering as we passed beneath the Golden Gate Bridge. I laughed, hardly able to believe I'd finally made it. I decided to tour the famous city for a few hours before heading down to Los Angeles, but when we disembarked, its streets were cold and gray. Los Angeles, though, was sunny and warm. I saw the brightness of orange groves as we reached the shore. I buzzed with excitement and could not sleep.

The next morning, I climbed aboard a Greyhound bus en route from Los Angeles to Indiana. With only two hundred dollars to my name, I was afraid to spend money on food and ate a single

---

For the first time, I felt free. And as the sun rose over the vastness of my new country, I gazed out the bus window and thought again of the girl with the red shoes, and how much I wished she could see what I saw.

---

candy bar in the three-day journey. I was hungry and tired, but I sat upright, watching Route 66 roll by for hundreds of miles through deserts, mountains and plains. Every time I closed my eyes and slept, I woke to a new and different landscape, each one stamped with the reflection of a free Michiyo in the window.

For the first time, I felt free. And as the sun rose over the vastness of my new country, I gazed out the bus window and thought again of the girl with the red shoes, and how much I wished she could see what I saw. I thought: *I am already rewarded for following the call of my heart.* My burning desire for freedom from a violent home and a stifling society had led me down a long road—even across an ocean and two continents—to find that freedom had always lain within the deepest, truest part of my being. My real journey, it turned out, was to discover that nothing and no one could limit my possibilities but myself.

Today, to all of the people I work with who hail from the United States and all over Asia, the Middle East and Africa, I am Dr. Michiyo. My psychotherapy clients know that I understand their struggles. And they know I am dedicated to helping them find their own inner paths to freedom. Inspired by my farm-girl angel, I hold a vision for their great possibility and invite them to try it on—like a pair of beautiful red shoes.

Michiyo Ambrosius, PhD, psychologist, author, yoga instructor, and personal coach, was born in Tokyo, Japan. She left Japan on a search for freedom, and now helps others rise from the depths of despair and locate the true freedom that lives in their hearts and souls.

Michiyo graduated from the University of Illinois in 1968 with a degree in audio-visual communication. In 2000, she received a PhD in clinical psychology from Pacifica Graduate Institute. Currently, she works as a clinical psychologist and personal coach in private practice. As a certified yoga teacher, Michiyo teaches yoga to senior citizens and incorporates yoga postures and breathing techniques into psychotherapy. She hosts workshops on yoga, meditation and dream work and is working on a book, Cultivating Wisdom through Midlife. *She has also published a CD recording of guided imagery called* Healing Touch. *She lives with her husband in Northern California. Connect with Michiyo at www.DrMichiyo.com.*

Renee Featherstone

Mr. Right

He was perfect. My friends called him Mr. Wonderful, but to me, he was Mr. Right. Since childhood, I had dreamed of marrying Mr. Right, having Right kids and living righteously ever after. Not in my wildest dreams would I have considered that Mr. Right would show up as an old acquaintance. Back in those days, we were both happily married to other people and admired and respected each other's relationships. Years later, when both our relationships had gone south, we bumped into each other at a nightclub. It was great seeing David and catching up, and we made plans for lunch the next day. Little did I know that lunch would eventually turn into a vibrant, loving relationship.

David was a catch. He was tall, dark and handsome for starters, but more importantly, he was intelligent, considerate, loving and compassionate. We connected in a deeply spiritual way. Maybe it was luck, maybe something else, but I had hit the Love Lotto jackpot. I know my opinion of him was biased, but it seemed that everyone who knew him loved him—my friends, family, and most importantly, my five year-old daughter. My girlfriends wanted him cloned so they could have one just like him.

About a year after we started dating, David asked me to marry him. Because I'd been married twice before, I wasn't sure about walking down the aisle again. Yet I had never loved anyone so fearlessly, and because he loved my daughter and me so unconditionally, I said, "Yes." My daughter was overjoyed when we told her.

Over the next nine years of marriage, our relationship grew and our family bond deepened. We had a strong foundation of love and respect. David and I had different religious beliefs, but before long he adopted some of my spiritual practices and even became an administrator and spiritual practitioner at my church. We meditated and prayed, cooked and played together. We were on a magic carpet ride. I shared with my friends, "Marriage is fabulous when you marry the *right* person." I coached others on the value of honest communication for a successful relationship. Communication was a theme in our household.

Even at age fifteen, my daughter was always forthcoming and willing to share details of her teenage adventures. So it was no surprise one night, as we sat in the car preparing to go in the house, when she said, "Mom, can I talk to you about something?"

Over the next nine years of marriage, our relationship grew and our family bond deepened.

"Of course, honey," I replied. "I'm all ears." She seemed a bit uncomfortable, but I was ready for anything. Or so I thought. "Um, well," she said, "I feel uncomfortable around David." I heard her words, but I couldn't comprehend what they meant.

Denial kicked in—there must be some misunderstanding. She then went on to describe inappropriate ways he had touched her, held her, watched her. He had molested her. Something exploded in the pit of my stomach. *How long has this gone on? How did I let this happen to my baby? Why didn't I notice something? How can I protect my child now?* So many questions flooded my mind, and yet I knew I must focus on breathing and thinking clearly for both my daughter and me.

That moment was like my own personal 9/11. My world as I knew it collapsed. David had committed what felt like a terrorist act—an act of violence and destruction on our home, our family and my heart. Just this morning I had been madly in love with my soul mate. Now it was as if my daughter and I lay on the side of the road in a state of shock. Through all the confusion, I was clear about three things: my daughter and I must confront David; we could not stay another night under the same roof with him; and I would have to report my husband to the police.

I insisted my daughter confront David, with me there to back her up. I wanted her to reclaim her power, hold her head high, and never consider she'd done anything wrong. In the presence of my

> My head was spinning. My Mr. Right
> had become Mr. Nightmare.

daughter, he tried to laugh it off, saying, "Oh, well, you're older now. I'll have to act accordingly." *Accordingly, what the hell does that mean?* I refrained from exploding out loud for fear I wouldn't be able to stop myself and David would end up in a hospital. I needed to stay focused on getting my daughter through this. When I confronted him alone, he admitted it, tearfully confessing he'd molested his own daughter when she was this age. My head was spinning. My Mr. Right had become Mr. Nightmare.

The police said he fit the profile of a classic pedophile. Often they marry someone with a small child, and build trust until the child reaches the age they prefer. My daughter was fifteen. His daughter had been fourteen. The police informed me that he had a past record of allegedly sexually assaulting a thirteen year-old. It felt like the air had been sucked out of the room. I could not breathe.

It came down to my daughter's word against David's. With a police phone tap, my daughter could call him to get some proof on tape. I refused to put my daughter through that, and volunteered to make the call. The police informed me that it would be most effective to meet him at a public place, wearing a wire. If I was willing, they would have two undercover cops back me up. I was willing. I could not allow another child to be his prey. At this point, all of David's attempts at reconciliation had fallen on my deaf ears. So when I called and said, "I'm willing to meet with you if you are willing to be completely honest," he eagerly agreed. Over lunch, I insisted, "I need you to acknowledge that you molested our daughters." It wasn't easy getting him to admit it, but when he did, I felt triumphant.

RAPED! I thought, TWO women? Who is this person I was married to for nine years?

I went on to inquire about the thirteen year-old. Almost with pride, in his defense he blurted out, "That is not true! I have only forcibly raped two women in my whole life!" *RAPED!* I thought, *TWO women? Who is this person I was married to for nine years?*

How could Mr. Right be so wrong? Was I so blinded by love as to not be able to see these things? What about our family and friends and members of our church—were they also misled by his charming façade? It seemed David was just extraordinarily skilled at deception. Was any of what I shared with him over the past nine years real, or was it all an illusion adeptly sketched by a social deviant?

I'm sure those hours I spent sobbing in my car, my shower, my bed and on my therapist's couch helped to wash some of the emotional debris away. But it was the long talks with my daughter, our therapists and God that pulled us through to the light at the end of the tunnel.

A year passed and with it went many moments of depression and fury. I was determined not to buy real estate in Victimville or on Hate-'em Lane, so I looked at my incredibly strong daughter and declared, "We now have a choice to make that will impact the rest of our lives. We can allow this to be our life story, and never trust, love, be free or take risks again. Or we can decide that despite what happened, we will commit to living our best life from this moment on."

Martin Luther King, Jr. said, "You don't have to see the whole staircase. Just take the first step." Sometimes it felt like we were taking one step forward and two steps back, but we kept on stepping. I learned to forgive myself and we both learned to trust again, love again and live again.

Almost ten years later, my daughter is a college graduate with her own business, and is in a healthy relationship. She has chosen not to hide her experience of molestation in a dark closet of shame but to use her life experience to counsel and support friends. With her as an example, I constantly remind myself of the power of choice—to trust and have an open heart so my blessings can continue to flow.

I've learned to celebrate my life, to know that I must be "Ms. Right" for myself first, that my daughter is the Right child and that we get to redefine "happily (righteously) ever after."

Renee Featherstone is an empowerment coach, facilitator and speaker. She helps individuals and groups by engaging their minds and hearts to move them to new realms of possibility and action. Ms. Featherstone coaches individuals toward the goal of making peace of mind their regular state of mind. Currently, Ms. Featherstone is facilitating personal growth and empowerment seminars for men, women and teens through her company, Into the Light. She has worked with prison inmates and foster-care teens, and has been awarded a Toastmasters International Best Speaker award. Connect with Renee at www.ReneeFeatherstone.com.

Helen M. Dela'Houssaye

From the Ashes, I Rise

As I sit in this cold, funky, dirty place, I wonder, "How did I get here?" *Where is my life? Is this what I'm destined to do?* I watch the other female inmates parade around in their orange jumpsuits, laughing and socializing like we're at a 5-star resort. *Why aren't they upset? They're in jail!* The other inmates are pros— going to the bathroom in public on the white dingy pot like it's nothin', playing games in the cell, laughing and enjoying the food. They are right at home here in jail. *There is no way I'm getting used to this. Jail may be home for them, but it's just a pit stop for me.*

As I wait for my hustlin' partners to get me out, I think about the last time I felt this low. Laying flat in a hospital bed, covered in bandages, the first face I saw was my grandmother, Mrs. McBree. She held a little pink bundle, my baby girl, Heaven. My husband, a Marine who said that he loved me, had beaten me into a coma.

After my recovery I wanted to feel alive, to do something, anything! So I left my grandparents' home and got my own place. My grandmother didn't want me to leave. After fighting to save my life, she worried someone might harm me again, or that I would harm myself. Before I left, she placed something powerful on my heart. She said, "Helen, greater is he that is within than he that is in the world. Never lose faith, baby."

Soon after leaving, I made a phone call that would change my life—the phone call that would eventually lead me here, to jail. I called my brother. My mama's side was different from the safe, strict home I had been raised in. My brothers, sisters and cousins always had something exciting going on. I remember watching my brother from the window—the smoothest brotha on the block—

When he answered, I said, "Hook me up with whatever ya'll are doing! I'm down." I was in. Just like that.

---

strutting around with a big wad of cash in his pocket. I didn't know the mean world he operated in; I just knew he had nice things and money to burn. When he answered, I said, "Hook me up with whatever ya'll are doing! I'm down." I was in. Just like that.

I was in over my head and didn't even know it. All I knew was I could make ten thousand dollars just driving two packages across state lines. *What! Ten thousand dollars?* You know I was trippin! I couldn't put gas in the car fast enough. For a twenty-year-old woman with two babies, this was lottery money. With a car filled with gas and a trunk filled with drugs, I began my first journey into the underground world.

My love for the fast money got me into everything. I sat down my standards and picked up the hustler's way. For the next ten months, you name it, I did it. Selling drugs, extortion, fake ID's, unemployment check schemes, even prostitution. I was even setting the scene to be a pimp over my own group of prostitutes. "Helen is crazy! She's lost her mind! She is doing unthinkable things!" I knew the stories about me were getting back to my grandparents, and it was breaking their hearts. I worried that the pain I caused them would kill them. But I couldn't be stopped. I was the Real Deal!

The day I got caught was a day like any other. "Delah, you gotta run this package down to Jacksonville," my brother said. "Same ole thang, nothin' different. Pull over at the rest stop right off the state line, put the package in the bathroom in the trashcan and cover it up. You got that?" I had done it so many times before, I thought, "I got this thang down, I'm living the life."

As soon as I crossed the state line, it was like Christmas: flashing lights and noise all around me. Police cars swarmed my car, helicopters roared overhead and before I could think two thoughts, a thunderous voice said those words you think you only hear in the movies: "Come out with your hands up!" K9 dogs sprang into action and found the package almost immediately. I got out of the car, my hands raised high, and it seemed like a thousand gun barrels were pointing at me. I almost wet my pants.

Right at that moment, my heart racing, my clothes drenched in sweat, time seemed to stop. And yet, everything happened so fast. My palms were clammy and my legs shook uncontrollably. It felt as if I could not find my breath, as if someone named Fear and Panic came and snatched the air from my body. All I could do was pray. "Please, God, if you give me another chance, I will do whatever you want me to do."

Would God listen to a hustler like me? I wasn't sure if I had the right to pray, let alone ask for my life to be saved. Still, the little girl inside me who was always there, desperate for love and acceptance, rose up in me and screamed for protection.

Feeling those cold, hard handcuffs around my wrists, and the cold, hard looks from the officers, I knew there was no acceptance, no love, no fame, no glory. The Drug Enforcement Agency (DEA) had been trailing me for *months*. They knew I was dealing with a lot more people, people who played a bigger game than I did, much bigger than my small ten-grand run. They questioned me for hours as I sat on a hard metal chair. My butt felt like I had been sitting on jagged rocks for three days, my mouth felt like cotton and my insides pained me from hunger.

And now here I am, sitting in a cold, damp holding cell, in so deep I have no idea how I'm going to get out. My bail is set at one hundred thousand dollars. You hear me? *A hundred thousand dollars!* I can't even imagine what that kind of money looks like.

There's no way I'm coming up with bail. My desperation is so strong, I can feel it running through my veins. *Where's my brother? Where are my partners? Don't they know I'm on lockdown and I need them to come bail me out?*

I wait. And wait. And wait. No one comes for me. *They just used me. They cashed in on my hunger for fast money and used my ignorance to their advantage.* Who will help me now? And then I realize it's time to make another phone call.

My hand shakes as I dial the number I know by heart. As the phone rings I say a silent prayer, holding out hope that this call will change my life as the call to my brother once did. But this time, I hope the people on the other end will do more than change my life. This time, I hope they will save it.

I call my grandparents, and steel myself as I prepare to tell my grandfather the truth. "Daddy, I'm in jail. I've been charged with drug trafficking and possession. I'm lookin' at fifteen years and I need you to post bail so I can get back to my children."

But this time, I hope the people on the other end will do more than change my life. This time, I hope they will save it.

I brace myself for his response, knowing he'll be angry, but that he'll also say it will be okay, they'll get me out. Click! *What was that? I know he didn't just hang up. The phone must be broken.* I hear the sharp click of the line disconnecting, and then the dull hum of the dial tone.

I feel like I've been punched in the gut. *You've done it now, girl, you have burned your last bridge and you are goin' straight to prison.*

The next morning, my grandparents come to the jail. When I see their kind, warm faces through the thick glass window, I breathe a sigh of relief. I notice the fingerprints of other inmates who had pressed their hands on the glass, reaching out to their own loved ones, their own saviors, hoping for a second chance. *I want my second chance, or my 200th chance. I don't care how many chances I've blown, I want another.*

"Please don't leave me here. I can't live like this. I know I turned my back on you. I know I caused you great pain and shame, but this has rocked my world and now I really want to get out of this game. Please, I'm begging you to help me get out." His eyes

---

"Even though I know you're guilty, I'm going to let you go, young lady, because you're going to tell your story to others, and you're going to make a difference in their lives."

---

more frighteningly stern than the officer who arrested me, my grandfather says in a clear voice, "I have a man you need to speak to, and you do whatever he tells you to do—you hear me, gal?" Without hesitation, I nod. I am overjoyed. *My grandfather hasn't written me off.*

As he walks away, a tall black man walks up and introduces himself as my lawyer. Later, standing before the judge, he paints a picture of my life. "Helen is a young woman who has endured molestation as a child, was raped twice before her eighteenth birthday, is the mother of two children, and was beaten into a coma by her husband." As he shares the whole, ugly story of my life, I shudder. He says I have Post-Traumatic Stress Disorder (PTSD). I was living with it, but I had no idea what it was.

After hearing the case, the judge examines all of the damning evidence against me. I feel my grandmother's prayers from across the room as my grandfather braces himself to hold her up in case I am found guilty. The judge shakes his head; the evidence does not lie. He leans back in his chair and says, "Even though I know you're guilty, I'm going to let you go, young lady, because you're going to tell your story to others, and you're going to make a difference in their lives."

The words ring in my ears as my grandparents reach for me. God gave me one more chance. *I'm going to let you go.* The judge's words are like a magic spell, waking me from a deep sleep. And that's when I realize: I may have recovered from my husband's beating in body, but my spirit had remained in a coma all these years. It took being locked up in jail for me to realize I had been in jail all along.

I didn't realize then that the story wasn't over yet, that I was going to learn how to fall really hard and get back up. I would learn how to turn my crawl into a walk, and my walk into a run before I finally learned how to soar. I was soon on my way to turning my entire life around and would one day share my humbling story of fate, focus and determination with thousands of aspiring entrepreneurs.

My mission is to teach through all of my life lessons. That day in court, the judge must have heard God say, "Let her go. This child of mine has much work to do! She will show my children that you can go through a living hell, survive it, understand it and then show other people how to *not* make hell their home. Hell is only a pit stop on their way to greatness!" And I thank God that the judge listened.

Known as "The Network Mogul," Helen M. Dela'Houssaye is a motivational speaker, life coach and author. Although accomplished in her corporate career, Helen aspired to be true to her inner conqueror and joined Ardyss International, a leader in the wellness and reshaping industry. Today, with more than 200,000 people in her downline and a million-dollar business, she is one of network marketing's most inspirational success stories. Helen travels the globe teaching and motivating other conquerors to generate wealth and live their dreams. She shares her proven tools in her signature "Ardycation & Motivation" workshops. With Omar Tyree, The New York Times bestselling author, Helen is currently writing a motivational book, Do You Believe: 21 Lessons Before Success. Connect with Helen at www. HelenDelahoussaye.com.

Mike and Amy Cornelsen

Landen's Legacy

Curled up together on a small couch in the empty hospital waiting room, wishing we could lay flat, we find a few moments of sleep. Up all hours feeding, rocking and changing diapers, parents of newborns rarely sleep through these first, dreamlike days after a child is born. Right now, we would give anything for a typical sleepless night caring for our son. Instead, we wait for news. Will he live?

Less than twelve hours before, Landen Michael, our second child, was born full-term and apparently healthy. We eagerly waited to hold our baby boy as the nurses tended to him. Then the doctor muttered something about his color change. And abruptly, just minutes after Landen came into the world, he and the doctor left the room. We assured ourselves—it was probably nothing. No cause for alarm.

An hour passed, and we were finally able to see our son. He rested peacefully, but connected to several tubes. At almost ten pounds, he had a frame that we imagined would put him on the starting line of a high school football team one day. He'd probably be a varsity wrestler too, just like his dad. The doctor interrupted our reverie. Something was wrong; Landen's oxygen levels were low and he would have to be moved to another hospital. A midnight ambulance ride later, Landen was diagnosed with a form of congenital heart disease. The major arteries of his heart were transposed, a condition that prevented oxygenated blood from flowing to his body through his heart.

Now, in the dark, we pray for our son as the cardiologist performs a balloon septostomy, an operation that should allow circulation of enough oxygenated blood to sustain his life. Somewhere in this hospital, our son's life is in the hands of a stranger.

I grasp Amy's hand. I remember meeting her in high school. I was captain of the speech and debate team, but when I met Amy, I was speechless. I felt instantly connected to her, and never argued when she decided we were going to be best friends. And now my best friend, my wife, needs me more than ever before. What can I do to

---

Yet inside, we pray. Inside, we believe. Inside, we hope.

---

make this easier on her? A few hours ago she chose to check out of the hospital where Landen was born and make do without postnatal care for her recovery, rather than remain behind. Now this hospital will not admit her as a patient. She copes with the pain without complaint, but the only relief I can offer her is Tylenol borrowed from a nurse's purse.

We wait. We pray. We believe he'll live.

I swallow three Tylenol tablets, my first pain medication since giving birth. My body aches, but it's my heart that's breaking. There was no way I was staying behind, left to wonder what would happen. Mike is amazing. He consoles me. He acts as my nurse. He is my best friend.

The doctor smiles when he walks in. "He made it," he says. We both let out a sigh of relief and say a silent prayer of thanks. "But he's not out of the woods yet." Still, we think, he's okay. We'll all go home soon.

We are admitted into a nearby Ronald McDonald house for families with children in the hospital, and finally get the chance to call our two year-old daughter, Leah, who is staying with friends from our church. Then, at last, we sleep. Not long after, though, we are awakened by a phone call from the hospital. "It's not looking good," the neonatologist says, in a grave tone. "You should come back to the hospital."

When we arrive, we see that Landen's skin, partially hidden under wires and tubing, has turned a dark shade of purple. There is no clear explanation for this—the operation should have saved his life—but now his only remaining option requires moving him again, to Children's Hospital in Washington, D.C. "He was fortunate to survive transit the first time, and he's weaker now. This may be the last time you see him alive." Yet inside, we pray. Inside, we believe. Inside, we hope.

While the nurses arrange transportation, I hold him for the first time. I sit in a wooden rocking chair with Mike standing behind me, his arms around me, and together we cradle our son. I'm still recovering from childbirth, and pain shoots from my lower body up through my back and stomach. Still, I don't move. I'm afraid if I even shift my weight, this moment will break and I won't be holding him.

Now, in the neonatal intensive care unit at Children's National Medical Center in D.C., we try to sleep in another hospital waiting room while Landen endures yet another procedure, his last option. He is connected to a machine that oxygenates his blood artificially, but at the risk of causing bleeding in his brain. If he makes it through this and stabilizes, he can heal.

My stomach hurts so much, I can't sleep for more than a few minutes at a time. I start bargaining with God. "Lord, if you let Landen live, I'll never miss another day of scripture study again."

Again Landen survives, and again we are warned he could pass on at any time. We are admitted into another Ronald McDonald house, and this time we begin to recognize our own pain on the faces of other parents. From their body language, we can see some couples growing closer from the experience, and some couples falling apart. Sharing our feelings, our love for each other deepens. Landen's vital signs strengthen.

We sing a children's hymn to him, "I Am a Child of God." We make sure our moments together are uplifting. Amy regularly pumps and freezes breast milk, anticipating the day Landen will be healthy enough to nurse.

And then it happens. As we stand by his bedside, his eyes open! He blinks, and we see his spirit in his big, gorgeous, blue-gray eyes. We hold hands, awed to finally witness the totality of this child we've created, our angel son. Landen keeps his eyes open for several precious minutes, and then closes his heavy lids (the effect of days of sedation).

Each morning we are grateful that he has survived to see another day and that we are not alone—we have each other. As each milestone passes, we stay positive about his chances for recovery. Our feelings mirror the EKG screen—up, down, normal, up, down,

---

And then it happens. As we stand by his bedside, his eyes open! He blinks, and we see his spirit in his big, gorgeous, blue-gray eyes.

---

normal—but still, we have hope. The doctor pulls us aside. "I'm not sure you understand how serious this is," he says. "We may just be delaying the inevitable."

It seems we are so unfailingly optimistic, so unwavering in our belief that Landen will one day come home from this hospital, everyone is concerned for us. They think we're in denial. "They seem to have pessimism covered," Amy tells me. "It's our job to have hope."

"A bleed has developed in Landen's brain," the doctor informs us a few days later. "We have to remove him from the machine and see if he will survive on his own."

We hold hands once more as the doctor explains, yet again, that Landen may not live. We are told that even if Landen survives, his brain has likely been permanently damaged from the bleeding. It is unlikely he would live a normal life, and we would be burdened with his care.

We go to the temple seeking solace, to tell the Lord we will accept Landen however we can have him. We leave with a clear impression that we must accept the outcome, whatever it may be. At three in the morning, the hospital calls. "His organs are shutting down." Now we understand; this is not a coincidence. Landen held on until we were ready to accept his true mission: to come into our family and allow us to experience the miracle of his life, and the miracle of his return to the Lord, thus focusing us on eternal life.

We hold vigil with him through the early morning. When we finally sign the waiver, they disconnect the tubes and wires, except one connected to his pain medication. We hold him in our arms together, both of us bent over him, rocking and sobbing. We tell him, "We love you, and we release you. Your mission on this earth is complete." Twelve days after he was born, Landen's little heart slows down and then, finally, stops. We gently lay down his body and, knowing his spirit has already departed, we leave too.

Mike holds the van door open for me, ready to leave the Ronald McDonald House. I stand staring blankly, tightly holding the bag of bottled breast milk I'd been preparing for Landen's first feedings. Can't we keep just one bottle? Mike wraps his arm around me, and I cry, knowing that bottle will never be used. Finally, I drop the milk in an ordinary garbage can, and we make the long drive home with an empty car seat.

Now we are beginning to truly live again.

We listen to each other all the way home, and we hold each other all that night. We cry together when we put his unused bassinet in the closet. We cry with family and friends as we welcome them to the funeral. And then, together, we lift the wooden casket that protects his still body and carry it to its resting place.

A few weeks after our family has returned to their homes, I notice we have just talked about Landen without crying. This gives me an idea. "We are going to have couple time tonight," I announce.

69

"What's that?" Mike asks. "I don't know, I just made it up. But it's going to be our new nightly tradition, and it is going to be fun."

Choosing to recreate one of our favorite dates from high school, we bake chocolate chip cookies. We talk. We smile. We laugh. Now we are beginning to truly live again.

Months later at the public library, a woman sees Leah and exclaims, "What a doll! Is she your only child?" I hesitate, and in a moment I relive it all—the twelve days of uncertainty and pain we felt as we watched him slip away. But with the pain came a gift. The gift of deeper love and commitment to our marriage, our family, and our purpose in life. The gift of knowing we are stronger than we ever imagined. And as that commitment and knowledge continue to grow, so does our connection to Landen.

"No, she has a little brother," I reply. "A girl and boy, how perfect," the woman says. Filled with a sense of peace, I reply, "Yes, yes they are."

Mike and Amy live in Englewood, Colorado, with their children, Leah and Camden. They treasure the unique aspects of their roles as husband and wife: parents, co-authors, business partners and best friends. Connect with them at www.MikeAndAmyCornelsen.com.

Jana Samulski

The Magic Closet

I'm flying through my neighborhood on my Big Wheel, pedaling furiously, taking turns wild and fast. The wind blows and lifts my curly hair all the way up into the clouds with the birds, my companions. They call down to me and I chirp back in response, taking a hard turn left to stop, nearly flying over my tiny wheels. I lift up my hands to the heavens and cry out: "Oh, Mighty Isis! Oh, Mighty Isis!"

The Secrets of Isis was the very first super-heroine show to air on TV, in the 70s, right before *Wonder Woman*. Wonder Woman may have needed an invisible jet to get around, but Isis was a full-fledged goddess able to command all the powers of heaven and earth. In *Isis,* a science teacher on an archaeological dig in Egypt unearths a mysterious box. Inside the box is a magical necklace, an amulet that imbues her with all the extraordinary powers of the goddess Isis. And when she chants, "Oh, Mighty Isis!" those powers are activated.

I was always the tiniest kid in school, a fragile slip of a girl standing last in line and never picked for kickball or other games. I also had what was then considered a strange first name, and my kindergarten teacher pronounced it incorrectly through that entire year; I was too painfully shy to correct her. My last name, Crum, earned me further bullying and ridicule. Every day I heard, "crummy, crumb cake!" or "she's smaller than a crumb," or "speck!" Their jibes pierced my little heart like arrows, but I never said a word. I kept to myself, stuck in the outsider identity my classmates pinned on me. I had no confidence at school, no self-esteem, and generally played alone.

But that all changed when I went home. Because at home, I had the magic closet. Just to the right of our laundry room was a huge, walk-in utility closet, and in this closet, I would transform myself from "crumbcake" to superhero. It was a safe, empowering little space to build dreams and let my imagination soar. In my

---

When I put on the amulet, I felt truly powerful. I wasn't just as strong, as beautiful and as gifted as Isis; I was the great Isis herself.

---

magic closet, surrounded by paper goods, antique linens, pet food and other cast-off items not ready to be thrown away, I could be whoever I wanted to be. I would shut the door, change into my Isis dress, put on my homemade tinfoil cuffs and *become* Isis.

As Isis, I commanded the elements; I could talk with animals, move objects and act as a champion of truth and justice, defending the oppressed and unfortunate. My strength was legendary.

The magic closet also served as a kind of stage from which I would leap, chanting the words that enacted my transformation, with hands outstretched. I imagined a poor little girl stuck in a tree, and flew up to save her. I chased down phantom bank robbers and reprimanded them. Full of mythic power, I mimicked the graceful movements of JoAnna Cameron, the actress who played Isis. Something about the way she moved was both enchanting and utterly self-possessed. *She would never be called speck,* I thought to myself, as I imagined myself twirling in her flowing white dress.

Dressing the part of Isis was a very big deal. Some nights I would stay up past my bedtime and sneak back into the magic closet to prepare ensembles, indulging in the self-confidence just *being* in the magic closet gave me. I loved Isis's necklace best, the amulet of power. My mother had a necklace that reminded me of it, and she let me wear it when I pretended to be Isis. This thrilled me. *I could do anything if I had a REAL amulet of power,* I thought. When I put on the amulet, I felt truly powerful. I wasn't just as strong, as beautiful and as gifted as Isis; I was the great Isis herself.

Though still timid at school—with nothing to be done about my peanut stature—I began to attract other girls like myself who suffered because they didn't fit in. At about age six, I befriended Michelle, a little girl from Japan. Because her skin was a different color and she spoke a different language, she met with even more derision from our schoolmates than I did. I invited Michelle and other friends to my house to play with me inside the magic closet, and together we would transform into Isis, Wonder Woman and other goddess-like superheroes full of personal power and unyielding strength.

Perhaps it was Isis who influenced me: I gravitated toward the underdog girls in every phase of my childhood and teenage years. We "last-picked" were seen as a group by the others because we were rejects, but we actually did identify with each other. We each understood what the others were going through. At the same time, we found each other more interesting and fun to play with. I knew that, like me, my odd-girl-out friends harbored some pretty wonderful secret powers: we knew how to reinvent ourselves.

But I didn't know how to carry my transformational powers with me into the real world, and soon I outgrew the magic closet. I got through high school okay, but in college I felt like "crumb" again, even though no one actually called me names. I just couldn't take the pressure; I couldn't find that inner confidence I had tapped into so easily playing Isis. Though I still don't how I managed to flunk every class, I got straight F's my first semester in college. I was devastated—I had failed before I really even started. I wondered, *would I ever have the confidence to succeed, to take my place in this world?*

My parents yanked me out of college immediately, and I got a job waiting tables. This time, my skinny frame garnered unwanted speculation from my peers and co-workers. "She must be a cocaine addict," they would say under their breath as I walked by. "You know she had to move back home because she failed all her classes—must be drugs." The rumors weren't true, but soon I found myself pretending they were. I assumed the role of "party girl" and stayed out late, drinking and dancing with friends, trying to fit in. I knew in my heart I was a good person, but I couldn't get it together.

Soon, my life was a pattern of lame jobs and cheating boyfriends. In my mother's eyes I saw concern and pain. I knew she worried

I was devastated—I had failed before I really even started. I wondered, would I ever have the confidence to succeed, to take my place in this world?

I was headed down a slippery slope. She was right—I was. In the eyes of my friends' parents I saw a different look: disapproval. I wanted to say, "I'm really a good girl. I'm just a little lost."

After I waited tables for a year, my parents helped me get back into college, with a light load of classes to help build my confidence. When I was twenty, I applied to an international study program in Salzburg, Austria, and was accepted. *No one will know me there,* I thought, excited at the prospect of escaping my loser status, the rumors and my "speck" of a life, and reinventing myself in Europe.

So I left my old life behind and started a new one in Salzburg. In Europe, no one knew I had failed all my classes or that I had become a party girl. My confidence grew as I learned to converse in German and mastered all of the nuances and taboos of this foreign culture. I got it *all* down. In Austria, I was forced to look at myself as an American through the eyes of Europeans. I began to redesign my appearance, my voice, my mannerisms, all modeled after the Europeans I interacted with every day.

Like my old magic closet, Europe allowed me to reclaim my power, but this time, as an adult in the *real world*. Emboldened and inspired, I studied behavior, communication, how people interact—my first step in becoming a master of these skills. When I came back to the United States many years later, I had become Jana. Crumbcake, the scrawny little speck, was nowhere to be found. And this time, when I stepped out of my "magic closet," I took my newfound powers with me.

I was forty when I finally started my business of teaching people how to put together the pieces that make them powerful beings. When I did, my mother sent me a gift. And when I opened the box, my breath caught: in it was a beautiful East Indian amulet necklace. Touching it, I smiled and whispered, "Oh, Mighty Isis." The necklace looks just like the necklace that Mighty Isis used to wear on TV, like that treasured piece of my mom's that I first used

---

I think my amulet is a symbol of the enduring part of me, the powerful woman I have always been, but maybe didn't always know I was.

---

to turn myself into Isis in the magic closet. It is a touchstone, an amulet of my very own power. I think my amulet is a symbol of the enduring part of me, the powerful woman I have always been, but maybe didn't always know I was.

As a shrimpy little kid, I commanded the power of a great goddess. I pretended so passionately and so often that the feeling took root—like I was trying on my true identity. I see the same kind of transformation take place with the people I teach: when they dress and act the part they want to play, that's the part they get. After a while, they become accustomed to being who they were always meant to be.

The magic closet was my refuge, my transformational haven, and I may never have discovered it had I been born with a "normal" name, of "normal" size, with "normal" abilities. Who wants to be normal when you can be a superhero?

As an expert speaker, trainer, radio host and author, Jana Samulski teaches people how to use their appearance, behavior and communication to get anything they want out of life. Jana has an international education and career from Europe and the United States in the fashion and corporate communication industries. The Jana Samulski Company delivers speaking and training expertise for such clients as Sony, Cushman & Wakefield and PricewaterhouseCoopers. Association and institutional clients include the National Association of Personal Financial Advisers (NAPFA), the Building Owners and Managers Association (BOMA), YMCA, LA Fashion District and Metro. Connect with Jana at www.JanaSamulski.com.

Ella L. J. Edmondson Bell, PhD

One of the Best Things

My junior year, I learned that Arthur Prysock's daughter, Jenora, was also at my college. Arthur Prysock was a great jazz musician whose voice could make girls do what they weren't supposed to do. Jenora and I became friends, and one Friday night, she invited some other friends and me to her house on Long Island. Me, at Arthur Prysock's house? I couldn't wait to tell my brother.

We sat in the elegant living room, laughing and talking. Jenora's mother, Jean, came out with a tray of soda and chips to welcome us. She smiled beautifully as she approached, but when she saw me she stopped and dropped the tray. Chips and soda spilled all over the rug. *That was about me,* I thought, and grew quiet.

Later, after everyone else had left, I talked with Mrs. Prysock in the kitchen. "Excuse me, ma'am, you looked at me very funny and then dropped the tray," I said. "What was that all about?" "You reminded me of someone I knew when I was your age," she said. "Who was it?" I asked. "You wouldn't know her." I pressed her. Finally, she said, "Jeanette Johnson." Shocked, I said, "That's my godsister." She was stunned for a moment, then said, "Your godfather is Joe Johnson?" I nodded.

That white-skinned black woman got even whiter. "When was the last time you saw your godsister?" she asked. I told her I'd never met her. "You need to meet your godsister," she said. "Soon."

Then she added, "Has anyone ever told you how much you look like her?"

I found out I was adopted when I was four. I didn't know what the word meant before then, but I did know I was different. Mom and Dad were a lot older than my friends' parents. My brother, Arthur, was old enough to be my dad. I didn't look like any of them, either. Mom was fair-skinned, with straight, pale hair; Dad was brown-skinned with chiseled features and wavy hair. Blue-eyed Arthur was so fair that his Army certificate listed him as white. I was honey-red brown with frizzy long hair and a wide nose. I did not mind that I was adopted. I thought it made me special. Out of a whole big batch of babies, someone chose me.

She smiled beautifully as she approached, but when she saw me she stopped and dropped the tray. Chips and soda spilled all over the rug. That was about me, I thought, and grew quiet.

I grew up in the South Bronx. My godfather, Joe Johnson, and his wife, Jenny, lived in Brooklyn. I wasn't allowed to visit their home, but they visited me on Christmas and my birthdays. They always brought me a beautiful doll. I spent one summer at their house on the Jersey Shore. They had a daughter, Jeanette, who was my godsister. Everyone said Jeanette was beautiful, but I never got to meet her. By the time I'd grown up and entered college, I'd almost forgotten about Jeanette. But then Jenora's mother sparked my curiosity again. Who was this woman who looked just like me? I had to meet her.

Thursday nights, my brother always joined us for dinner, so I waited until then to tell the family about my visit to the Prysocks. At a table filled with my brother's favorite food—fried chicken, pinto beans, biscuits—I coyly said, "Guess where I was last weekend?" My brother asked where, and I said, "Arthur Prysock's house." He was excited and jealous. "Was he there?" "No, he was on the road," I said. We all laughed.

Then I casually added, "I've got to call Godfather. Mrs. Prysock knows him and Jeanette. She said I looked just like her. Nobody's ever said I looked like her. I've got to meet her." A darkness suddenly descended over the room. My father put his head down on the table, and my mother got up and paced. No one looked at me.

What was happening? In total confusion, I watched the lines deepen on my mother's forehead. After a long silence, Arthur said, "You better tell her. She's about to find out, and it's better to hear it from you."

The next words from my mother's mouth had the power to collapse a thousand buildings. My mother, always so stoic, and yet now visibly nervous, looked up and said, in a stone-dry voice: "Joe is really your grandfather. Aunt Jenny is your grandmother. And Jeanette... she's your mother."

I felt the betrayal physically, like someone had just cut my heart out or punched me so hard in the stomach I couldn't see straight. I doubled over in pain, and when I straightened up I could barely see past the steam of anger rising from my body. I went off on everyone at that table, in ways they couldn't have imagined; I called them everything but "Child of God." "I can't believe this sh##t! What the hell is going on? You all betrayed me. You're all liars. If you've been lying to me all of these years about who I am," I yelled, "then I can't believe anything you've ever told me, including that you love me."

I was furious with my family for keeping the truth from me, but I was also enraged with the Johnsons, high-yellow folks with their summer house, private schools and fancy cars. They had it all, while my family struggled to get by. *So I wasn't good enough for them? Me, the child they chose to hide.* "They're not good enough for *me!*" I shouted. "Especially Jeanette. She never even bothered to seek me out! That selfish bitch." I threw my plate across the room, breaking it against a wall. "Enough's enough," Dad said. I rushed out of the house, angry, bewildered and hurting beyond repair. When I came back later that night, I didn't know who I was anymore. *Who do I belong to? Was I chosen because I was adopted, or was I given away?*

My confusion took up real estate in my head for years and years—from city to city, through schools and universities, as student and teacher, through a marriage and so many men—as

> *My confusion took up real estate in my head for years and years—from city to city, through schools and universities, as student and teacher, and through a marriage and so many men—as I tried to find myself, a place where I belonged.*

I tried to find myself, a place where I belonged. Because I felt I couldn't trust the people closest to me to tell me the truth, I couldn't really trust anyone. I failed at building meaningful relationships. Because I never believed anyone when they said they'd stay, I'd sabotage my relationships by testing the waters every which way I could—I'd push and push and push and push, until they finally left and proved me right.

I compensated for my relationship insecurities with my intellectual achievements. By the time I was thirty-eight I was a Yale professor, working on a study comparing white and black women in corporate America. As part of the study, I took a cross-racial team to see a photographic exhibit of African-American women from all walks of life at the Finch Museum in New York. At the museum, I ran into Jenora Prysock. We hugged and caught up, and I asked after her mother. "She's over there," Jenora said.

I walked over to Jean. "I don't know if you remember me," I said. She smiled warmly. "Oh, I remember. You're Jeanette's daughter. I knew that the night I saw you." Even twenty years later, it hurt my heart to hear the words. I'd spoken to my mother only once, thirteen years earlier, just after separating from my husband. I asked Jean if she knew where my mother was. "Last I heard, she was in Mexico. She's ill, and they won't let her out because she's written bad checks." My mind screamed. *What? My mother, ill?*

A criminal in Mexico? The information overwhelmed me. I broke down in the museum, crying my eyes out.

A few months after my breakdown in the museum, I phoned Jean Prysock. "I need to find Jeanette and see if I can help," I said. Jean told me to write a letter to the family, and said she would make sure it reached a cousin of mine. Then, before Thanksgiving, Jean

---

Maybe I had always been where
God meant me to be.

---

called back. "I've got some news," she said. "You need to sit down." She told me that my mother had died in Mexico. Shocked and confused by my emotions, I sat paralyzed. It was doubly painful because my adoptive mother had passed away earlier that year, in June. And now I'd lost both the mother I knew and loved, and the mother I would never know.

One year later, I got a phone call from Jeanette's cousin in Las Vegas. My letter had been passed around the family until he finally received it and had the courage to call me. "We all knew Uncle Joe had a goddaughter, but no one understood why there weren't any pictures of you," he told me. A warm feeling filled my soul just knowing that they wondered about me. We talked for hours and told each other about our lives and families, and he invited me out to Vegas to meet everyone. My great-aunt Edna—Aunt Jenny's baby sister—was going to be there.

In Vegas, I met so many relatives who were excited to meet me; I was thrilled to meet my very own family. They all said I looked and laughed just like Jeanette. Aunt Edna told me so much: Jeanette had been a teacher, a wanderer and a smart woman who never got the chance to use her voice. Edna told me how hard it was for Jeanette to give me up, and that Jenny insisted she do so to save the family from shame. She told me how Jeanette nursed my grandfather until he died, and how she took her other daughter to Mexico to attend law school and escape racism in America. This was my family tree, sprouting reasons and clarity.

"So she gave me away," I said, in the voice of both a woman and a little girl. Aunt Edna shrugged. "It was the wrong place, the wrong time, and the wrong family to be a single mother in. Beyond that, I just don't know." I felt both her love for me and her pain for my experience.

As a scholar, teacher and advocate studying and fighting against injustice toward minority women, my awareness of betrayal had grown, over the years, from my own story to the story of society. I was a wounded healer, and my own wound had not yet healed.

When I heard my mother's story, I finally began to understand: Jeanette's betrayal had not been personal. As a young adult, pregnant and out of wedlock, born into in a family trying to transcend racism through social status, wealth and propriety, she never had a chance to keep me. And she'd never recovered from the difficulty of her journey to find freedom in society.

Maybe I had always been where God meant me to be. Thinking I was an unworthy, unwanted child, I forgot that I also came from a long line of esteemed DNA. It blessed me with the capacity to be productive in professional academics, and to use my position to build an organization for women of color so they could make a difference in their lives. I don't think I could have done it without knowing Jeanette's story, my story.

Later, when Aunt Edna was dying, I got to her bedside just in time. Tears ran down my face; I was about to lose my favorite relative besides my own parents. She turned her head to me and smiled. "I'm glad you're here," she said. "When I get to heaven, I'm going to tell my sister that the worst thing she ever did was give you away." I cried even harder. *I belong to this woman and her family,* I thought.

Then she said the last words she ever spoke to me: "You're one of the best things to happen to this family." I believe her.

*Ella L. J. Edmonson Bell, PhD, is the founder and president of ASCENT—Leading Multicultural Women to the Top, and an associate professor of business administration at Dartmouth's Tuck School of Business. She is considered a leading expert in the management of race, gender and class in the workplace; PepsiCo, American Express, Intel, Goldman Sachs and the U.S. Department of Labor are among her clients. She is the author of many articles and two highly acclaimed books—*Our Separate Ways: Black and White Women and the Struggle for Professional Identity *and* Career GPS: Strategies for Women Navigating the New Corporate Landscape. *Learn more at www.CareerGPSTheBook.com.*

Dr. Zari Alipour

My Life Is My Own

My teacher handed me my achievement certificate, and I took it with shaking hands. Trembling with excitement, I read the results: twenty out of twenty on my final exam. I had just graduated from the sixth grade with a perfect score, at the top of my class. I ran all the way home and burst into my house. I handed the certificate to my mother and father and breathlessly began to tell them my plans for my future.

My father interrupted me. "Education is not a good thing for a girl. You can read and write and that is good enough." He handed me back the certificate.

All the air was sucked out of my frail little body. My mind simply jammed. I couldn't speak. I went into the other room and sat down in a chair. When I was finally able to calm my swirling thoughts, I gritted my teeth and whispered to myself, "No. You cannot control me."

I had always been a sickly, fragile Iranian girl, living in the shadow of my younger brother, longing for the acceptance of my authoritarian father. My mother was simply a passive presence in my home, neither a support nor a hindrance; she just followed my father's orders like the rest of us. Now that had changed. I had been forbidden to go to school anymore, but I remained determined to educate myself—somehow.

I was a twelve-year-old girl. The only plan I could muster: make some money and hope for a miracle. It wasn't much of a plan, but it was something. I finished sixth grade in May of 1966; that summer I started working strategically on my goal, in secret. I hung a note on our front door: "Sewing jobs accepted." Why I picked this I still don't know. My experience as a seamstress was limited to making clothes for my dolls when I was small, and a white and pink button-down dress I had stitched together a few years earlier. When customers came calling. that dress was my one and only

---

"Education is not a good thing for a girl. You can read and write and that is good enough."

---

advertisement. I'd meet them at the door wearing it and smiling confidently. Amazingly, it worked.

Although my mother knew what I was doing, she never commented on my new occupation. She was content to be the shadow in my life. My father, on the other hand, said it was "an excellent way for a girl to keep busy." With my first paycheck, I went out and bought the textbooks I would need for the seventh grade. I never opened them, just kept them nearby and always within sight. I knew that, someday, I would go back to school and the books would be there. This went on for two years. I was making good money. But still I was in need of a miracle, some way to get around my father's barrier. It came from the most unexpected place.

One of my uncles had a brother-in-law who was a teacher. One day, while I was visiting my uncle, this brother-in-law happened to be there. "What grade are you in, Zari?" he asked. It was like a knife puncturing a balloon inside me that had been growing with all of my unspoken dreams. I broke down in tears, and my story poured out of me. When I had finished he said, "Would you like to go back to school?" I stared at him through a veil of tears and managed to utter a single word. "Yes." My first miracle had arrived.

The first step, he explained, was for me to obtain a written medical excuse from a legitimate doctor explaining why I had missed two years of school. My grades were excellent, so that put me in good standing, but during that time in Iran—even though the society was very Westernized—it was going to be difficult to get readmitted to school after being away for such a long time. *I needed another miracle.*

During those years, I was often plagued with migraine headaches, so I used them as my excuse to go visit a doctor. As I sat in the doctor's office, staring at my thin hands and wondering how I was going to convince him to write the letter, the door opened and he walked inside. "So what appears to be the problem, Zari?"

Again, it poured out of me. "My father has forbidden me to continue my education. I've been making money and looking for a miracle to return to school. I know a teacher who can help me, but it all depends on you writing a note for me." He stared at me in disbelief and then asked, "How have you been making money?" "Sewing," I answered, and bowed my head, expecting ridicule. But

---

I looked up. He was crying. He wiped the tears from his eyes and placed his hand firmly on my shoulder. "I will write whatever you need me to write if it will get you back into school."

---

he said nothing. I looked up. He was crying. He wiped the tears from his eyes and placed his hand firmly on my shoulder.

"I will write whatever you need me to write if it will get you back into school."

My second miracle had arrived. I prepared a package including the doctor's letter and presented it to the teacher I now called "My Guardian Angel." In October of 1968, he presented the package to the school and I was instantly accepted. My grades had been that good. And amazingly, the school that took me in was the one I had dreamed of attending for many years—the Sapar School. My joy was indescribable.

And yet I still I had to keep my education a secret from my father. I told my mother, but as always, she offered no words of encouragement or disappointment. Hers was always a quiet support. But it was my father's blessing that I yearned for most, even though I knew it would never come.

I stepped within the school walls and looked around me; it was as if I had stepped into one of my own dreams. My heart pounding with excitement, I wore my white and gray-striped dress, and clutched those books I had bought years ago proudly in my arms. My first class was math. The teacher, Mr. Magd, smiled down at me: "We have an exam planned for today, but you, of course, won't be required to take it." "I love math!" I screamed, beaming with joy. "I'd be happy to take it!" He laughed. "Okay. But I won't hold it against you if you don't do well." I received one hundred percent on that exam, the best grade in the class. *I had arrived.*

For the next three years, I went to school—and continued to keep it secret from my father. After school, if he happened to be

---

I looked up. My father was at my side. He helped me stand, then gathered my papers and books and placed them gently back into my hands. And then he embraced me. "It's okay," he said, "I know."

---

home, I dropped my books at a neighbor's house and retrieved them later. I stopped my sewing jobs and replaced them with tutoring jobs, mostly with my own classmates. I asked them not to come to my home, but one day my father caught me. I felt a fist form in my stomach, and prepared for the worst. But amazingly, he was more puzzled than angry. "How does a girl with only a sixth grade education tutor eighth graders?" I simply shrugged and walked away. I felt as if I had just tutored my father.

My boldness and self-confidence continued to grow. One day, I was on my way to school with my head uncovered, wearing suspenders and a sleeveless dress I had bought with my own money—the entire ensemble scandalous for a culture in which women were expected to be modest. He stopped me at the door and said, "Look at you! Dressed like that!" I turned to him and set my feet. I was committed to not being another version of my mother. I told him very clearly, "This is my body. You cannot control me." I walked out on shaking legs, but I was smiling. Later that night, my father acted as if nothing had happened.

I was in the ninth grade and walking home from school with my books and papers clutched against my chest, feeling happy and confident, when I looked up and saw my father watching me from the other side of the road. I stopped. He stared at me. I lowered my head and kept walking, trying to remain calm, but my heart began to drum inside my chest, the world began to spin and I lost my balance and fell. My books tumbled to the concrete and my papers spilled out, scattering everywhere. I looked up. My father was at my side. He helped me stand, then gathered my papers and books and placed them gently back into my hands. And then he embraced me. "It's okay," he said, "I know."

A lifetime of fear and anger just vanished. *He had been afraid, just like me.* We never spoke about it again; I went away to college, wondering if this brave step would be too much for my father to handle. But on my first day at university, I received a package from him. Though there were no words of encouragement, no mushy notes, in it was the one thing he could give me to show me that he believed in me: money, for me to buy my books—and with it, acceptance. The most sacred miracle of all had finally arrived.

Dr. Zari Alipour is a licensed psychologist, a certified alcohol and drug counselor, a clinical hypnotherapist and a neuro-linguistic practitioner, all in the state of California. She is also a member-in-good-standing of the Los Angeles County Psychological Association, the California Association of Marriage and Family Therapists and the Los Angeles Counsel of School Nurses. Connect with Zari at www.DrZari.com.

Door Number Ten

Ten doctors sat around the table in a large, chilly conference room lit with harsh fluorescent lights. They all wore white coats with their names written in illegible blue cursive letters over their hearts. The combination of scribbles that passed for names and the distance they kept from us made everything incomprehensible; and as we greeted the doctors and made our way to our seats, my husband and I immediately felt ill at ease. What unfolded was like a TV game show, only instead of ten doors behind which might lie great prizes, here sat ten doctors, each poised to give a report.

We were at a major university children's hospital. At many large medical institutions, there's a protocol by which doctors are trained to keep their distance while still making an attempt to forge a relationship with you. Today their blank faces and averted eyes created a chill in the room, a foreshadowing of the quiet before the storm.

Three and a half years earlier, I'd given birth to my beautiful son, Jamison. He was our first child, and the first grandchild on both sides of the family. We were all, predictably, ecstatic. As he approached his second birthday, we noticed that he didn't talk like others his age. While other toddlers used two words to make demands or express feelings, Jamison got by with one-word utterances, and even those were often hard to understand.

My husband had graduated from Harvard Law School and worked in a top Philadelphia firm. I had graduated from the University of Chicago and was an executive in a major pharmaceutical company. We were high-achievers. Worried as we were, we had to remind ourselves not to inadvertently place our high expectations for ourselves onto our son. All kids, we told each other, develop differently.

When my son was three and a half, we took him for his regular checkup. It was clear then that we could no longer "explain away" his speech deficiencies. During the routine checkup, Jamison's

> *What unfolded was like a TV game show, only instead of ten doors behind which might lie great prizes, here sat ten doctors, each poised to give a report.*

pediatrician expressed concern about his speech, saying he needed a full evaluation to rule out serious deficits. We scheduled Jamison for a week of tests at the university hospital. Three weeks later, we sat in a chilly conference room to get the results. This was the game show.

Doctor number one buzzed in with, "You have a lovely boy. He's engaging and very happy." Doctor number two buzzed in: "We've evaluated his speech, and while he has difficulty speaking, there's nothing wrong with his ability to form words." *What does that mean?* I thought. *He can speak but he can't speak?* All of their niceties contradicted the weight of their tone. The doctors continued, and with each new report, my frustration and anxiety grew. *What are you trying to say? Please tell me exactly what is wrong with my son!*

On all game shows, the tension mounts near the final rounds when the stakes are highest. This was no exception. The doctors continued to buzz in, each report just adding to the confusion. I gripped the pad I was using to take notes and saw the sweat from my hands staining the paper. I was out of my element, no longer an executive running a meeting, but a scared mother unsure if I truly wanted to hear any more of the confounding reports.

But what was behind door number ten? After an hour, doctor number ten buzzed in for the final round. "Mr. and Mrs. Potter," he said, "we have concluded that your son has autism." The room went silent as the diagnosis hung in the air like a bad smell that couldn't be waved away. My husband and I were stunned into a moment of shocked, pained silence. This was twenty years ago, when most of what we knew about autism came from TV documentaries where the most severely affected kids sometimes wore helmets to protect themselves.

With the mother in me at a loss for answers, I leaned on my years of experience in the medical industry and launched a battery of questions. "What causes autism?" I asked. "We're not sure," someone said. "Is it diet? Trauma at birth?" I persisted. "We're just not sure." "What can we do now?" my husband asked. "You can do

---

Finally, exasperated by our questioning, one doctor blurted out, "Mr. and Mrs. Potter, I don't think you understand. Your son will never even be able to place an order at McDonald's!"

---

early intervention," one doctor said. "That consists of small classes for your son or even one-on-one help." "Where are the people who can help?" my husband continued. "We can give you some names, but there aren't many." Ten doors, ten coats, ten medical degrees, but no real answers or promises of help.

The diagnosis threatened to change every dream that my husband and I had for Jamison's life. All we wanted was a strategy for helping our son, and a prognosis. We needed to know where all this was going to lead our son and our family. But rather than the direct answers we needed, we got a lot of dancing and wasted time. My heart aching, I scanned the room for clarity, understanding or just a glimmer of hope—but most of the physicians sat completely quiet and stared down at the table. This was just another day at the office for them, but our family's future hung in the balance as our heads swirled with questions. Finally, exasperated by our questioning, one doctor blurted out, "Mr. and Mrs. Potter, I don't think you understand. Your son will never even be able to place an order at McDonald's!"

My husband and I sat in complete stillness as the cruel comment burned onto our hearts and into our minds. Were we to dampen our expectations and hopes to match the physicians' belief that little was possible for our precious son? *Who the hell are you?* I thought. *Your training doesn't make you God! You have the power to diagnose my son, but you don't have the power to determine his destiny!* Blinded by our agony and lost in our grief, my husband and I gathered our notes and steadied our legs as we made our way to our car.

On the long drive home, my husband and I were utterly silent. The pain of what we'd just been told ran too deep. And I was pregnant. To add to our pain, we'd learned from the doctors that it wasn't unusual for parents who had one child with autism to have a second with the disorder. When we returned, I held my beautiful little boy, feeling so grateful to be in the safety of home. But I was still absolutely devastated. In an odd way, I felt I had been duped. Jamison was just as sweet as he was when I had left that morning to meet with the doctors. But he was no longer the little boy I thought I knew.

I couldn't get over the sense that my son was an impostor, a different little boy that I would grow to know all over again. My feelings of betrayal, fear and hurt didn't affect my interactions with my son; my struggle was internal, in my mind and my heart. But my typical, composed self, the me that always had the answer and the strategy to resolve most any challenge, was completely disoriented, lost and scared.

Through a blanket of tears I whispered, "Who are you?" But even as I asked the question, I knew who this child was. He came from my womb. I knew him—and yet, I didn't.

Our lives changed overnight. My husband and I withdrew from the world and put our life on hold as we mourned intensely for months. Family outings, and the routine Sunday brunches we had regularly hosted for close friends, were now few and far between. Our whole vision of Jamison's future was in flux. We could no longer assume that he was going to be an Ivy League lawyer like his father, or a business executive like me.

> *As we finally accepted the diagnosis, we stepped fully into our job as parents: to help our son be the best at whatever life led him to do and ensure he felt great about himself, regardless of the challenges he might face.*

But we had to separate our mourning from the work that needed to be done. We immediately enrolled Jamison in special developmental sessions five times a week, coupled with special work done at home with the same frequency. Our family life consisted of twenty to thirty-mile drives to therapists so Jamison could get the language, social, play and physical therapy he needed. At home we made games of flashcards and word drills, communicating by drawing pictures when words weren't getting through. We also created our own solutions when the established methods failed. This routine lasted for years, and though managing it all was like having second full-time jobs, we found time where previously we thought none could possibly exist. As we finally accepted the diagnosis, we stepped fully into our job as parents: to help our son be the best at whatever life led him to do and ensure he felt great about himself, regardless of the challenges he might face.

Our daughter, Lauren, was born four months later, and we lived in uncertainty for another year. She didn't show signs of being affected—she talked constantly from an early age—but for the longest time we just weren't sure. With each developmental milestone she reached, we sighed with relief. We knew we loved and cherished Lauren no matter what, but we lived with the fear that we would have two autistic children. At twelve months old, wanting a treat, Lauren said her first sentence: "Cookie me?" At that moment I knew in my heart she was okay. Still, we needed the assurance the doctors would give us six months later.

Within a few years I felt better, both from the passage of time and the progress Jamison made. His therapies had a measurable effect; he recited the alphabet, printed letters and numbers and expressed himself with multiple-word sentences. The day he learned to tell time was one of the most joyful days of my life. I saw my deep belief in my son matched by his hard work, resilience and results.

As my pain lifted, I found my gratitude again. I was so grateful to Jamison for being a precious, loving son and for the lessons he taught me through our experience together. My whole life, I had said that we're all the same and that God loves us all. But when faced with the possibility of my boy setting pins in a bowling alley for a living, I was forced to confront the arrogance inherent in my definition of a high-achiever.

Jamison graduated with honors and an Associate's degree from a California college, and is now working toward a BA. And he doesn't place orders at McDonalds; he much prefers Chinese take-out. He has many gifts. But his primary gift to me was to help me see that the true definition of a high-achiever is someone living with an open mind, a grateful heart and a purposeful spirit. Jamison is no impostor. He's my son—wonderful, talented, educated and mine. Behind door number ten is my perfect child.

Myrtle Potter is CEO of Myrtle Potter Media, Inc., and Myrtle Potter and Company, LLC. Myrtle is widely recognized as "The Trusted Voice in Healthcare." Connect with Myrtle at www.MyrtlePotter.com.

Marcy Cole, PhD

The Heart Whispers Truth

"We are ready to go now," said the charismatic rabbi in his Russian accent. I had just signed the *ketubah,* the traditional Jewish marriage contract, and as the rabbi signaled it was time for our wedding ceremony to begin, I suddenly burst into tears. Earlier that morning, surrounded by bridesmaids, I had felt lighthearted anticipation. But in this moment, the soulful tears streaming down my face felt like a visceral outpouring I could not suppress.

To pull myself together enough to walk down the aisle, I took a breath and focused on the beauty of everyone dressed in white, like angels. *That's the reason for the tears,* I told myself. *I'm simply overcome.* I focused on the rabbi's words, meeting my cues, Henry's face, the love and warmth emanating from our family and friends.

After the ceremony, I laced my arm with Henry's—but the videographer captured a different story than the one I told myself that day. Our expressions were flat, and our faces looked drained; the camera could not lie. Beneath my veil was a deeper one...a veil of denial that was too painful to consciously admit.

Slipping into a private room for a few moments alone, Henry and I compared notes like two old friends. "Did you see so and so?" *Why aren't we gazing into each other's eyes?* "Did you see the flowers?" *Why aren't we focused on the sacred vows we just exchanged and the love we just expressed?* Despite the uneasy emptiness I felt, I let these thoughts pass. *Let's move on—it's party time!*

I practiced "moving on" and avoiding my nagging intuition from the moment our relationship transitioned from friendship to dating, during our senior year of college. My mind said, *Yes. I feel safe with Henry. He loves me, even with the extra twenty-five pounds! He's my "go to" guy for support. I miss him so much when we are apart. We have so much in common.* But my heart wondered, *Where are the butterflies? Where is the passion? Shouldn't I be more excited and certain about this?* We loved each other. I wanted to believe that our passion would grow.

During our early courtship, our relationship felt like a harbor of unconditional love, empowering me to lose the extra weight I had carried around since high school. But the bedroom was an entirely different story. *We're young. Shouldn't we be having sex all the time?* His therapist called it "normal performance anxiety." I called it frustrating beyond belief! *What's wrong?* I asked myself.

Beneath my veil was a deeper one...a veil of denial that was too painful to consciously admit.

Why doesn't he want me?

I stood by Henry while he explored the problem that was blocking him, and us, from having a healthy sexual relationship. After all, I was his safe harbor too. After countless intimate moments, we finally made love. But afterwards, my first thought wasn't *Wow!* or *Amazing, this is what I have been waiting for!* All I thought was, *Done, phew!*

After three years of dating, I knew it was time for me to venture out on my own in order to explore, expand and experience new horizons in my twenties. "I have to go," I told Henry. "We've been inseparable for years. Maybe one day we'll find our way back to each other." This time, I followed my heart and trusted my gut. Henry was heartbroken. I felt free.

We both moved on and dated other people. Henry moved to New York. In a wonderful, two-year relationship with Mitchell, I learned about adult sexual intimacy. *Finally, I feel alive and desirable!* Still, I found myself missing Henry and the comforting sense of security our friendship provided, especially when I felt disappointed or vulnerable in my relationship with Mitchell. A couple of years after Henry and I broke up, I heard he had a serious girlfriend. I felt pangs of loss, but not enough to leave Mitchell and go back to him.

But fate had a way of making sure I learned the lessons that destiny had in store for me. After Mitchell and I broke up, I inexplicably came across a phone message Henry had left three months ago. *How bizarre,* I thought. The very next day my friend ran into him. Ironically, Henry was back in Chicago, living just a few blocks away. He called, we went out, and then we just slipped back into the relationship.

We moved in together. Life was routine: get home from work, watch TV, eat dinner and go to bed. Our sex life was rote and infrequent, generally expressed on a Saturday night after a few drinks. Exasperated and hurt, I shared my feelings with Henry. "I am a passionate person. I want a passionate relationship, and I want to feel wanted!"

"You are just ambivalent by nature and idealizing everyone else's relationship, Marcy," he replied. This may have been bearable if I still had *my* Henry. But the generous, affectionate guy who had once been my biggest fan and staunchest advocate had become critical, aloof and withholding. When I shared my concerns, he blamed me: "You're the one who left. You need to be the one to prove your commitment." I believed him. It became my mission to "make this work," "right any wrongs" and "get the love back."

By this time, I was a pro at dismissing my nagging and terrifying feeling that we were seriously off track. I had experienced the withdrawal of love before, and grappled with the aching question: *Where does love go?* At the time, it was too painful to admit that this could be happening again—especially with the person who was once my best friend, most loyal and steady suitor and trusted companion. I was focused on securing the blueprint for my life and our future—marriage, a home and children. *I'm twenty-eight.... it's what every girl wants, right? And everyone wants this for me, and for us too. It's time!*

But the shortcomings of our relationship led me astray. I met an interesting guy named Don, who wooed me in all the ways Henry did not. Don drove eight hours to spend two with me, made me feel beautiful and offered absolute reason for pause. We spoke for hours on the phone and had a few unfaithful smooches.

But fate had a way of making sure I learned the lessons that destiny had in store for me.

One day I received a call from a delivery company, asking me to sign for a letter. Thinking it was for Henry, I sent it to his office. Henry came home and pulled an opened envelope from his briefcase. *Oh my God,* I thought. *This is from Don, and I actually sent it to Henry's office!* I could hear my heart pounding, and felt waves of fear and shame shoot through me. Henry's gaze pierced me as I read the words on the page: it was the quintessential love letter. Don professed his passion and pleaded with me to pack my bags and let him whisk me away. Pulling out all the stops, he shared a quote from the Torah that haunted me: "Before you marry, know whom you are going to divorce."

Overcome with guilt, I stayed with Henry. Despite our consistent unrest, I still felt pressure from him to get engaged. "Why do you want to marry me?" I asked him. "You're always unhappy with me. I don't get it!" A few weeks later, I walked into our home to find posters all over the house that listed "The sixty reasons why I love Marcy Cole and want to marry her." Henry always finessed big occasions with charm, generosity and bling, in this case a breathtaking diamond ring! When he got down on one knee, and said, "Will you?" I felt a flutter in my heart, a short breath of the exhale I had longed for, and simply said, "Yes."

Others perceived us as the perfect couple. But even after we married, life behind our closed doors continued to be fraught with the daily stresses of Henry's erratic moods and temper. It seemed some days he enjoyed being my husband; other days he resented me for accepting his proposal. Feeling consistently blamed and misunderstood, I tried to explain, defend, stay afloat. I was putting out fires all time, walking on eggshells, timing communications and hiding information. *I am only 30 years old and am already going gray!* My body responded to the stress with allergies, skin breakouts, and a back sprain. I reached out to alternative healing practitioners. One of them described the situation this way: "You are in a psychically oppressive relationship. Your husband's soul is sleeping."

"Before you marry, know whom
you are going to divorce."

I was still too paralyzed by fear to take action. Instead, I chose the route of intellectual distraction: my doctoral program. But I did make a comforting promise to myself: *I will not be in this place or feel this way forever!* In due time, I began to turn inward and asked myself, *What do you want?* The answer was *freedom*. I envisioned a partnership that would not define me, but would enhance a sense of ease and joy in my life. *I see my man walking into a room. He takes me in his arms and I feel safe, cherished and truly happy.* As I fully embraced my heart's desires, the ultimate question became: "Would I marry Henry all over again?"

No longer just a nagging feeling, the answer was clear: *Absolutely not!* I reflected on my wedding day, hanging on to the "leap of faith" hope of a life that was not meant to be. *I cried my way down the aisle that day because deep in the recesses of my heart, I knew I was going down the wrong aisle.* Now it was time to let go, have the courage to face the unknown and embark upon the path that would allow me to hear my voice, trust my heart and live my truth.

For years, I was terrified to speak of divorce. *What will happen to him? What will happen to me?* But it was time to take another leap of faith: *I will thrive, with or without a husband.* "We need to get a divorce," I said to Henry, holding my breath. His response brought forth a jolt of relief and a breakthrough for both of us. "I know," he said. We cried and held each other tightly, honoring the seventeen-year road we had traveled together. "I feel like I have you back," Henry said. A wave of peace washed over me.

Four months after our divorce, Henry invited me over for a night I will never forget. "I have something to tell you," he announced. I felt a shaking in my core, as I anticipated the clarity of his heart's expression. He exuded a sense of calm; yet there was palpable anxiety as he prepared to tell me the truth he had repressed for his entire adult life. Taking a deep breath, he said, *"I'm gay."* Our years of confusion, constriction and struggle flashed before me, as I remembered our darkest moments. *This is what it was all along... he was paralyzed by his greatest fear, which held the key to his ultimate freedom.*

At the age of thirty-two, I began to navigate my own journey. The past whispers of my heart became the foundation of my authentic truth, and that truth set me free. In doing so, it set my dear Henry free as well. In that, we are forever bonded, grateful for our entire journey together—every single solitary moment of it.

Marcy Cole, LCSW, PhD, is a holistic psychotherapist, workshop facilitator, author and speaker. Over the last fifteen years, she has developed an extensive private practice with adults, couples and families, integrating Western and Eastern perspectives on achieving optimal health. Dr. Cole's treatment process creates a safe space for personal reflection, re-evaluation, healing, discovery and manifestation. She offers consultations at the Wheel of Well Being in Los Angeles, California, and by phone. Connect with Dr. Cole at www.DrMarcyCole.com.

Sharon Brogdon

A Legacy of Mothers

I t was early Christmas morning. A fire blazed in the big stone fireplace, and the aroma in the air was a mixture of the earthiness of crackling logs and the crispy bacon that accompanied our traditional Christmas breakfast. Mom had been up long before us, cooked breakfast and started some of the Christmas dinner items that would simmer slowly, all day, on the stove. Everything was normal; everything was fine.

Except, Mom was keeping a big secret.

Doctors said the source of her nagging pain was only gallstones, but I'm sure she suspected otherwise. Her own mother had passed away very young from breast cancer, when I was a toddler. The long history of early deaths from cancer for the women in my grandmother's family must have weighed heavy on Mom's mind that Christmas morning as she determinedly did everything to ensure our holiday traditions went unspoiled.

Mom went in for her gallstone surgery as planned in January. "Nothing to worry about," she said as she showed me the twenty or so pearl-sized, lime-green and turquoise-colored stones they had removed. What Mom didn't tell me was that while performing this routine surgery, doctors had discovered something they couldn't just cut out of her: pancreatic cancer.

My mom swore my father and all our relatives to secrecy about her illness. Our education was a priority for her, and she was determined to ensure my sister and I didn't become distracted by her illness and lose focus in school. My sister was living on campus at a nearby university, and I was finishing spring semester prior to my senior year in high school. Right before that last Christmas, I had turned sixteen; had gotten my driver's license and first job; was on the varsity track team and trying to maintain both my grades and my social life. I was happy, in my oblivion, to focus on my day-to-day world, because Mom had said everything was fine. I'm still not sure whether I didn't pay attention to the signs or chose not to see them. I may simply not have wanted to face something being seriously wrong. It was too hard.

As months passed, Mom's doctor and hospital visits increased and she began to lose a noticeable amount of weight. She explained that she was receiving treatment for complications arising from spending so much time on her back during surgery. I loved seeing

---

Everything was normal; everything was fine.
Except, Mom was keeping a big secret.

---

her face light up when she opened packages of pretty new outfits I bought her, and I chose to focus on these happy expressions rather than the growing gauntness in her face and the increased amount of time she spent in bed.

Late one summer night, my father, a powerful yet quiet man, hurriedly bundled me into the back of the car and Mom into the front seat. I didn't know what was going on, but I knew from the sense of urgency in his voice not to ask any questions. As we sped off into the night in our large black sedan, I sat scared, quiet and alone in the back seat, watching the yellow emergency blinkers rhythmically click on and off as we rode swiftly in silence.

We ended up at the hospital emergency room, and my mother was immediately whisked away. My heart pounded as question after question flooded my head, but my mind refused to formulate answers. *Where have they taken her? Why have they taken her? Why are we here? Why won't anyone talk to me?* I felt so helpless and afraid—like a four year-old lost in a crowded mall. I felt so small in the midst of something so big, but no one could hear my frantic little voice. When my father collected me I searched his face for answers, but there were none. The two of us rode home in silence.

The next morning, Dad called me into my parents' bedroom. I sat on the edge of the bed, and he sat facing me. "Sharon, your mom has cancer," he told me. I sat frozen as my father's words hung in the air. I wanted to cover my ears and pretend I hadn't heard what he said, but my arms were so heavy I couldn't lift my hands to my ears. Tears involuntarily spilled down my face as my heart responded to the painful reality that my mind refused to acknowledge.

All the questions from the night before bombarded my consciousness, and the singular and ugly answer screamed in my ears. *Why are we here?* Cancer. *Why did they take her?* Cancer. *Why won't you talk to me?* Cancer. Cancer. CANCER!

My father's normally strong voice was soft and apologetic. "Your mother did not want you girls to be distracted from your schoolwork. She made me promise not to tell you that she was sick." He may very well have betrayed her confidence by telling me then.

On a hot September afternoon, just eight months after mom's original surgery, my great-aunt was scheduled to arrive for a visit. My sister made the thirty-minute drive to the airport to pick her up while I waited at home with her boyfriend. While we waited, my mother's doctor called twice and asked, "Are you coming to the hospital?" He urged us to come as quickly as possible. A small knot began to grow in my stomach, and it tightened as I detected the urgency in his voice. The doctor called a third time, but in this call, there were no urgent pleas to get to the hospital. He simply said, "Your mother is gone," and hung up.

My sister's boyfriend was right there with me. He could see from the disbelief on my face that the news was bad. I slowly hung up the phone, and for a moment, the room stood still. I felt as if I'd been punched in the stomach and had the wind knocked out of me. I couldn't breathe and my body was numb, yet I was acutely aware of my surroundings. The doctor's words echoed in my head very clearly, but I struggled to make sense of them. *How could she be gone? She said everything was going to be okay.*

As reality began to sink in, I crumpled into a fit of inconsolable tears. My suppressed anxiety, denial, loneliness and sadness—and the reality of that final phone call—were overwhelming. The emotional pain that enveloped me was intense. I felt as if my heart was slowly shredding apart, one agonizing strand at a time. That was the first time in my young life that I knew what it meant to

---

And with each of the life milestones that passed—graduating from college, getting married, becoming a mother—there were so many questions I wanted to ask her.

---

hurt to the very core of my being. My sister and my great-aunt came in the door a few minutes later and knew from my state that something was terribly wrong. When I told them that Mom was gone, my great-aunt immediately started pacing back and forth through the house, tightly hugging her sides and wailing, "Lord, Lord, I didn't get here soon enough—she died alone!"

Days followed in a blur. Family and friends came and went and arrangements were made. At the funeral, my sister and I were seated on the front pew. From there, I could see the fringes of Mom's hair and a portion of her face peeking out of the casket. After the service, we approached the casket to say our goodbyes. Mom had on one of her favorite dresses, a pink chiffon formal with crystal beading. She looked peaceful. I truly understood–my mother was really gone.

In the months and years that followed, I struggled with guilt that I hadn't been there for her the way I would have if I had known how ill she was. Well into my adult life, I overcompensated for my guilt by being there for everyone else, all the time, despite my own needs. I put those on the back burner—I'd never be so selfish again. I thought if I said "yes" to every request made of me, then I could band-aid my guilt with a feeling of service and selflessness. I wanted to make up for not recognizing my mom's needs. And with each of the life milestones that passed—graduating from college, getting married, becoming a mother—there were so many questions I wanted to ask her.

I needed an emotional breakthrough, and over time, through slow paths of healing, it came. As my ability to cope with the complete picture of my mother's ordeal increased, I realized that I could not be held accountable for what I didn't know—and as a carefree teen, I truly did not know my mother was so ill. As I accepted that truth, I gradually released my guilt and began to breathe again.

"Job well done, my beautiful daughter. My grandchildren are strong. Trust in their strength, love them and let them in. And be careful to not burn the bacon."

As my own children grew, I too sought to protect them from life's harsh realities. In doing so, I began to understand the decision my mother had made in an effort to shield my sister and me. She paid a huge price to protect us—that's what mothers do. We lay down our lives for our children. After all those years, I finally got it. I understood her decision. I also understood that the difficult choice she made framed who I am as a mother today.

Acutely aware of my own unspoken conversations, I talk with my children about everything and I've learned to trust in their ability to handle difficult news. We laugh together, we cry together, we cope together, and most importantly, we heal together. Even though my mother and I weren't able to have those life conversations at the kitchen table over coffee, she is still here with me in spirit. Now, as I rise long before my own family on Christmas morning to prepare our traditional breakfast, I can hear my mother lovingly speaking her guidance in my ear. In those quiet morning hours she softly whispers, "Job well done, my beautiful daughter. My grandchildren are strong. Trust in their strength, love them and let them in. And be careful to not burn the bacon."

A native of the Chicago metropolitan area, Sharon Brogdon is a speaker whose mission is to help working and professional moms enjoy the journey of motherhood. Sharon and her husband, Greg, are the proud parents of Christopher, twenty-three, and Kelli, twenty. Sharon is currently working on her first solo writing project, in which she shares how her experiences shaped who she became as a mother. Connect with Sharon at www.SharonBrogdonSpeaks.com.

Joan Perry

My Mama Taught Me Well. Yes, She Did!

There I was, sitting in the shoe department of Saks Fifth Avenue with my mother next to me, watching in enchantment as the salesman brought her pair after beautiful pair of gorgeous spiky shoes to try on. She smiled as her fingers lightly brushed the finely shaped leather. I loved watching her treat herself to something that made her feel glamorous, womanly and happy.

And wow, did she have that stunning long-leg look! My heart leapt—I was so proud she was my mama. She bought three pairs of Stuart Weitzman super-high heels that day, with her own cash. *Chu-ching! Now that's freedom!* As we walked along the streets of downtown St. Louis—"the big city," we called it—I watched her swing her Saks bags. The message that I saw was freedom: freedom to choose; freedom to like myself; freedom to love being a woman. This vivid image has remained with me, and I'll hold it, dearly, for the rest of my life. It was the day I decided I would be a girl with cash, too—just like her.

It was unusual in her day—the 1960s—to be a girl with cash, her own cash, that is. With courage, she grew even more cash as she started her own business. It always gave me goose bumps of pride when I drove down Main Street in my hometown of Decatur,

Illinois, and saw the big banner that read "Perry Travel." That business belonged to Mama.

When she went to work—that's when I saw Mama step up to be who she really was: a smart, accomplished, talented, creative and inspired woman. Work was what made her confidence shine and showed off her talents. And yet, there was the dark side—the secrets behind the outward success of my mother's life and the source of my pain. At dinner each night, there was a cruel ritual: my father would mock and insult my mother because she was vulnerable as she aspired in life.

Although my father, too, was accomplished, he let his jealousy rage, accompanied by glasses of wine: "You can't even balance your own checkbook, so you can't run a business." "Hurry up; can't you do it faster?" "Who do you think you are? You're not smart enough

---

It was the day I decided I would be a girl with cash, too—just like her.

---

for that." "No one likes you." "How come you spend all my money?" I wished that he would say something good about her. But on and on it would go, night after night at dinner. And what really hurt is that he would draw me into his tirade as his ally and make me laugh with him to mock my mother.

Others were jealous of Mama, too. I heard murmurings from people who resented her success. There were those who were quick to spread gossip and demean her abilities. This embarrassed and hurt me, because I wanted to have a mother that everyone loved. But through it all, she showed me how to step forward and live my dreams. She would whisper to me, "Don't worry about what other people say about you; it's when you are so unimportant that people stop talking about you that you need to worry." She said this over and over until it rang inside of me.

She was being tested—and she showed her courage. And it was both the rare glimpses of her happiness and the depths of her misery that taught me what it was to be a woman, taught me how to be a woman—how to tolerate unthinkable abuse and terror, while presenting "perfection" to the world outside.

I wasn't sure why I went to business school. Somewhere deep down, I must have known that it was a way out—a way out of the big hurt that plagued the inside of me. In my heart, I wanted to be loved most of all. Going off to business school was doing what I saw light my mother's happy spirit. It must be where I thought I would

> *Maybe, in being that girl, I would avoid the horrible agony my mother endured as I was growing up, and escape the secrets that both created my own pain and carved my own path.*

find the self-worth and pleasure that I couldn't find within. It was part of the legacy Mama created for me. And I loved the sound of the words, "I'm going to business school." It meant a journey to becoming a "girl with cash." Maybe, in being that girl, I would avoid the horrible agony my mother endured as I was growing up, and escape the secrets that both created my own pain and carved my own path.

As I graduated from business school and went on to a career in the investment banking world, I, too, was tested and nearly taken down by those who did not believe in me—just as I had witnessed my father trying to take down my mother. It was unsavory for a young woman on Wall Street in the early 1980s: "Sit up on the desk and spread your legs," and "I'll see that you don't have a job tomorrow." I faced what I had seen my mama face—and I found myself going it alone and hiding my fear, just as she had done.

The tricks and shenanigans of Wall Street, a place that didn't care in the least about me, ran deeper than this Midwestern girl had ever imagined. But I worked on being skilled—a solid, quick and clever negotiator—because Mama had taught me that living my vision was more important than the talk of the day. And I was determined to be a girl with cash.

One day, when I thought I'd seen it all, I was sitting at my grey metal desk in the middle of the testosterone-laden trading floor of the brokerage firm where I worked. The desks were so close together I felt I might suffocate—all I wanted was six more feet around my desk, and not human ones! My ears perked up when I heard a guy on the telephone at the other end of the floor say, "Be a pioneer, those are the ones with the arrows in their ass." I thought, Hey—here I am, the only woman on the trading floor—I *am* that pioneer!

And then I got it! I had to do what Mama did. I had to put on blinders, ignore the putdowns, the berating comments and the sexual insults to go forward and learn all that I could learn, all that I could soak up about all aspects of money. I had to do it in order to be able to teach other women, so they wouldn't have to suffer as my mother did. I was willing to be the pioneer, to set the stage, to gather the knowledge so that other women could have cash, too, to negotiate their lives.

I'd heard men say, "Women can't take risks." But my mama had shown me differently, as she grew her travel businesses to include her travel agency, travel school and various other enterprises that employed women. She eventually sold her business to AAA for a handsome sum. In my own time, I started the first female-owned municipal bond firm in the country, underwriting big blocks of bonds and selling them in the financial markets. I, too, proved that women could take risks.

So I learned about money, and how to teach others about it. I even wrote a top book about it, published by Random House. But while I toured to promote *A Girl Needs Cash*, I was holding a secret, just like my mama had; I had married an abusive husband. I was living in daily terror—holding my breath. One afternoon, while I was on a phone interview for a radio station, he stormed into my office in a rage, shouting that I had "a huge ego." I stopped the session immediately, and felt a blow to my stomach.

I was never comfortable anywhere I went to speak about my book again. Because I feared my husband's abuse, I dropped out.

Then and there, I stopped sharing my talents; I stopped the pursuit of my success dead in its tracks. Here I was, right back in the hurt that I had tried so hard to escape, and this time I was the focus. I withered and went quiet.

Not long after, my husband took his new girlfriend to the Bahamas (where I had taken him for our anniversary months earlier). Upon his return, he announced that he could do anything that he wanted to do (even though he was still married to me). I had put his name on my house, and we had other real estate assets together. As I gasped for air and cried in humiliation and anguish, I

I'd weathered abuse for being a strong and prosperous woman, but no more—I was finally done paying my dues.

---

flashed on my childhood. And then the divorce lawyers descended. What my husband didn't count on was that I had the tenacity of the woman who had gone before me: my mama, who had taught me not to be just a girl with cash, but even more importantly, a girl with assets. She taught me not to give up. I fought for what was mine, and I won.

Breaking free from my abusive husband and taking back everything that was rightfully mine—including my sense of self-worth—instantly reawakened my pioneering spirit, and my passion. I'd weathered abuse for being a strong and prosperous woman, but no more—I was finally done paying my dues.

As I walked out of the courtroom, I thought of Mama, happily, lightly stepping down the street in a pair of her new high heels. Even if she had taught me how to suffer in silence, she had also taught me to go for my dreams. And even if she had never escaped my father's tyranny, she had shown me what it meant to be free. I felt the glow of her pride in me.

Joan Perry is a president/CEO, author and speaker to groups of women. She is a leading expert on money management, and the unique perspective of women and money. She has developed her expertise during over twenty-five years as an investment banker working on Wall Street, as a money manager and as the owner of a securities brokerage firm. As President of Take Charge Financial!, Joan founded the first female-owned municipal investment banking firm in the United States, known as Perry Investments, Inc., in 1985. Throughout her career, she has managed billions of dollars in the bond, stock and options markets. Joan combined her personal and professional background in her book A Girl Needs Cash, *published by Random House in 2000—a story of money in women's lives and the transition to taking charge of it. Connect with Joan at www.JoanPerry.com and www.Facebook.com/JoanPerryAuthor.*

Tara Starling

A Beggar in a Queen's Castle

My legs gave out completely, and I fell with a loud, sickening thud into a crumpled heap on the floor. I couldn't tell what was stinging worse—my eyes, after nine months of relentless tears, or the scabs that covered my body, torn open from four solid months of incessant scratching.

My torn heart and my bleeding skin were in a contest to see which could bear the most scars. Although I had long since lost count of all the scabs, my heart held so many wounds that it was the clear winner. The incomprehensible pain of losing my husband, the life we had shared, and everything we dreamed of creating together was like an anvil the size of a planet sitting squarely on my soul, crushing, under the weight of my guilt, the thought of any existence beyond the endless cycle of tears and screaming. I had ruined my marriage and there was no way to salvage it. Happily ever after was no more.

I had just come home from the first counseling appointment I'd made to try to wade through the grief and loss I felt from destroying my marriage and losing my husband. Up until that point, I'd survived only by sheer force of will. Every day I woke up angry that there was still a beat in my heart and breath in my lungs. Only the knowledge that there was no way to die without causing grief and hardship for my family kept me alive.

Working on a movie set meant long hours every day with colleagues for whom I did my best to put up a front of steel-laced courage. *I have to keep it together.* I didn't talk about what was happening, or my former husband's last text: "Please don't contact me. Don't call me. Don't drop by anymore. Thanks." Until that day, I still wrapped my reason for living around my hope of salvaging the partnership I had destroyed. But when those final words blinked onto the screen of my cell phone, all the lights in the world went out.

My torn heart and my bleeding skin were in a contest to see which could bear the most scars.

My wounds were raw when I walked into the counselor's office, but I was hemorrhaging when I walked out. Reciting the whole saga to her, pulling everything out of the box, riddled me with the shot blast of a million screaming regrets. Everything I could have and should have done differently cut deep into my heart like the blades of dull, jagged razors. I just didn't know how to live my life anymore. I didn't even know who I was.

Now, my body stretched in prostrate defeat on the floor. The only thing that could have possibly painted another layer of horror on my life was lying squished up in a piece of toilet paper on the bathroom counter: an enormous, blood-engorged bedbug. For months I had thought my scabs were from heartbreak hives. But the reality turned my stomach inside out: an infestation of bedbugs had invaded my bed and my apartment. They had been sucking the life out of me, literally, during what little sleep I could find between the tears.

I looked at the smashed insect and saw my own grotesque reflection. All the fabulous trappings of my life had been shrouding the ugliness I believed to be my true identity—an ugliness I had believed so long that it became the lie I lived. I had lived like a queen, but in my heart I felt like a beggar and a fraud. Crawling up into a corner of the couch, I curled into a ball with my computer and searched all night for someone to save my home. I found a reputable exterminating company, called them the instant they opened, and watched a short while later as a specially-trained dog sniffed out the bedbug hiding places in my apartment.

"Leave everything," the exterminator said, "or they'll migrate with you." So an hour after they arrived, I stepped out into a gathering storm, wearing nothing but a sundress and flip-flops and carrying only my wallet, phone and laptop in a clear plastic baggie. In a second baggie, I carried Goliath, my baby tortoise. That night, I slept on Mom's basement couch, with little Goliath huddled beside me in his makeshift terrarium: a big blue plastic storage tub with a light bulb duct-taped to the side.

The bug-men couldn't predict just when I would be able to move back in; they could only say that the procedure would cost two thousand dollars. As I tallied the multiplying cost of these disasters, I felt the shadow of an unseen hammer looming over me, and heard a whoosh of air in my mind as it swung through the debris of my life to strike the anticipated final blow. It came quickly, in the form of a five-inch gash on the rental car tire the next morning. Of course, I had waived the insurance. My spirit hit bottom. I sat in the rented Chevy and wept. For the first time the words, "Why me?" fell from my mouth.

A horrible fear echoed within my soul: because of the hideous things I had done to lose the love of my life, I had also lost my calling. One of my deepest desires had always been to help free women from society's insidious lies about appearance, beauty and worth. Two decades as a makeup artist in the entertainment industry had given me some powerful insights and tools, and I longed to teach women how to claim and embrace their unique beauty. But I too had believed the lies about my own worth, and when I lost my husband as a result, I also lost all hope of ever creating anything beautiful again. Imprisoned as I was in the chains of my own guilt, I believed I was no longer the person who could share a message that would free other women. I was exiled now from both my home and my dreams.

But a week and a half after my exodus, a miracle occurred. I found myself sitting two feet away from where Lisa Nichols was standing, saying the words I had been praying to hear. "You have a message to share, and so you have been given the very experiences in your life which qualify you to help your brothers and sisters. Everything you have gone through is part of the Plan," she said, as tears of recognition rolled down my face. "You stand in the 'chapter twenty-four' of your life, but if you had not felt the pain of your 'chapter four,' you could not help anyone else get through hers and walk in freedom on the other side."

I felt a wave of joy. I saw a divine perfection crystallize. The anvil fell from my chest, and I could breathe again. After all my anguish, I could finally make out the faint outline of a master

> *Imprisoned as I was in the chains of my own guilt, I believed I was no longer the person who could share a message that would free other women. I was exiled now from both my home and my dreams.*

architect at work in my life. I could not help others cross through the darkness without having walked through it myself. Life as I had known it falling apart was necessary for the renovation of my soul. The walls I had lived behind had to be torn down to find the bugs that had infested my spirit.

I heard the whoosh again, and on the movie-screen of my mind I saw the giant hammer swing down, accelerating as it fell. This time, I saw that my raw and ragged heart wasn't the target, but a thick and moldy wall that encircled it. As the hammer crushed the stone, a rush of sweet air entered my lungs for the first time since I could remember. *The real me is in here,* I thought. *She's in here.*

The clearing of bedbugs from my apartment took another six long weeks, and in the meantime I leaned fully into the renovation of my soul, sensing now that underneath the wreckage of my life was a divine purpose to all the pain. I went diligently every week to counseling, trusting my doctor as she walked me though the healing process and helped me find and exterminate the lies that had been hiding inside my heart. It was hard to admit I needed help, but I knew I had to trust that it was part of the renovation process. I meditated every day, asking for answers to flow into the new spaces in my life.

Life as I had known it falling apart was necessary for the renovation of my soul. The walls I had lived behind had to be torn down to find the bugs that had infested my spirit.

One day, as I washed some dirt and debris from the crystals glued to Goliath's shell, the answer flashed across my heart. Beneath the grunge, the Swarovskis still sparkled. I realized that though my choices were all for me to learn from and had buried my light for a time, they didn't define who I was, or my worth. *I am not my mistakes! My destruction of my past does not negate the divinity of my purpose! Even if he never wants to see me again, even if my house is overrun with disgusting insects, even if I haven't got a cent, I am still worth living in a soul like a palace, instead of a cottage.*

When I knew what I was worth, my actions began to change. I fed my body the healthiest food I could find, and fed my mind and soul a daily diet of inspiring books and tapes. As I began to look at my reflection with love and forgiveness, my skin cleared up, and I shed the extra weight I'd been carrying around along with my self-loathing.

My eyes began to sparkle, my voice to sing; and I danced around the kitchen to Bach and The Black-Eyed Peas. My soul began to vibrate once again, and my heart finally began to remember joy.

And then the day came. It was time to go home. My tiny palace would be just as I left it, beautifully decorated in Tudor style, with rich tapestries, Gothic carved-wood chairs and crystal candlesticks. Every moment I had lived there before the exile, I had felt like a beggar in a queen's castle. *This beauty does not belong to me,* I had believed, *because of all the ugliness I've created.* Shame had populated my home with ghosts, pain and regrets. Though it was beautiful, it had been filled with the silence of sorrow.

Now, as I swung the door wide open, I saw that my home—and my life—had been whitewashed by grace. The shimmering light of possibility gilded every surface, and seeped into every corner of my soul. I knew, beyond all doubt, that I was worthy to receive all the riches, wonders—and yes, even love—that awaited me. I was home. And I knew that nothing I had chosen to do in my past would ever keep God from choosing to work through me, the moment I allowed Him to remodel, renovate, and remake my soul. The master architect had done His work. I had walked out a beggar, but I walked back in a queen.

Tara Starling is often described as The Joan d'Arc of Beauty. An international celebrity makeup artist for the last fifteen years, she has spent most of her life on stage and on set, working with some of the most famous people in the world and on some of the highest-grossing films in history. She opened a romantic boutique called Anastasia's Attic (www.AnastasiasAttic.com), and is the creator of "Star in Your Own Life," a transformational program which teaches women the skills and tools to live the role of leading lady in their own lives. Tara also established the About Face Foundation for Women, a non-profit which brings the truths and tools of transformation to disadvantaged women and speaks to women from every walk of life about finding—and living from—their own true beauty. Connect with Tara at www.TaraStarling.com and www.StarlingBeauty.com.

Monick Halm

After the Rupture

Blinking awake in my hospital bed after an emergency appendectomy, I felt a tremendous sense of relief. I ached, I couldn't sit up, I had nearly died—but I was relieved. It wasn't because I had survived this life-threatening illness, but because I didn't have to go to work!

When the doctors informed me that I would have several days of hospital stay, and thirty days of recovery at home to follow, I felt like I'd been given a vacation. "Something is definitely wrong," I thought, "if being in pain, in the *hospital,* is so much better than going to the office."

This was the first sign of its kind that I hadn't just dashed by in the rush and misery of my eighteen-hour days as an associate in a large corporate law firm. I didn't pay attention to my stomach aches as the clock spun and they got worse by the day. "I'll sleep when I'm dead," I joked, and ignored my body's rebellion against my breakneck pace and toxic career. It took an actual physical explosion for me to halt and reconsider my life. I was on the wrong path.

Always an overachiever and a good student, after I got my English degree I saw my only next step as law school. I didn't want to become a doctor, professor or engineer, and law was the one other career that meant success to me. I applied to, was accepted, and went to study at Columbia Law School, where I was one of the close to one hundred percent of graduates automatically spit out into jobs at major law firms. Was there an alternative? I didn't think about it.

Even in law school, my stressed-out body spoke to me through stomach aches. The doctor I saw for them at the university clinic said, "You're suffering from law school." I looked at him quizzically, and he said, "Your stomach aches are caused by stress. Try doing yoga." I did, and the stomach aches decreased dramatically. Even

---

"Something is definitely wrong," I thought,
"if being in pain, in the hospital, is so
much better than going to the office."

---

better, I began to understand them as a signal from my body to slow down and manage my stress. Years later at my job, however, I felt so overwhelmed that I simply stopped paying attention.

Not only did associates pull eighteen-hour days and even overnights at the firm on a regular basis, the partners we worked for heaped abuse upon us. Some yelled; some threw things. One partner never raised his voice, and yet every time I left his office I felt diminished to the size of a pea. Another had no sense of personal time and called meetings early on Sunday mornings at his whim. My fellow associates and I used to joke that we suffered from "Battered Associates Syndrome." We were at their mercy. And we took it for granted that we weren't supposed to be happy in our jobs.

Suffering and stress were part of the package, like the nice paycheck and a fair amount of prestige. *This is what I'm supposed to do. Maybe when I'm a partner it'll get better.*

In my precious time away from the glaring computer screen and fluorescent lights of the office, I cheered on a friend of mine as she competed in an ironman triathlon. Watching her, I got hooked by the idea of running one myself. It looked like so much fun! I signed up, though I didn't really have time. "I'll sleep when

I'm dead," I said, again. Soon, training became essential for my spirit—a grounding, joyful daily practice of running and bicycling on the beach in Santa Monica before heading into the office for the dreaded workday. Once a week I swam in the ocean, leaping in the sunny waves with the dolphins who often came to join me. The joy from those dolphins carried me through the morning, but by lunchtime my joy had already faded.

After six months of training, and with just a couple days to go before the race, my stomach started hurting severely. "These are not the usual stress stomach aches," I told my doctor, more than once, but he just kept saying, "There's nothing seriously wrong with you." Turns out I had built so much muscle around my appendix from the training that the infection remained relatively contained.

I finished the race (one-mile swim, twenty-five-mile bike ride, ten-kilometer run), barely feeling any pain because of the rush of adrenalin. But the next day I was back at the doctor's office. "I'm pretty sure this is appendicitis," I said, again and again. "I have a very, very bad pain on my right side." "That's impossible," said the doctors. "You couldn't have run a triathlon with appendicitis!" But sure enough, it was.

My appendix ruptured, and I was rushed into surgery. When I woke up, I really woke up. A friend gave me *The Artist's Way* while I recovered in the hospital. I worked with it and took my first deep, relaxed breaths in years; I felt my creative and spiritual sides crying out like starved creatures, waiting for me to feed them.

So I started meditating and, after the hospital, attending a place of worship. During my month of recovery at home, I walked on the beach, reflecting on the power of the ocean. I sat in the warm sand with my eyes closed, and drew energy from the sea. I began painting again, spreading color on my life again after many years away from art. I filled my patio with new plants, tending them with great care and attention.

For the first time, I simply followed what gave me pleasure. *My work is to feel this peace,* I thought. All things inauthentic fell away, and my life was transformed.

This month gave me time to reflect, too, upon the necessary change ahead of me. How would I manage it? What would I do? I knew that I had been on the wrong path. I had been busy trying to balance everything in my external world: job, social life, dating, training. I knew it was important to be happy, and that balancing my inner world was my first step to getting there.

A few months later, I got a call from a friend who was in Buenos

---

*All things inauthentic fell away,
and my life was transformed.*

Aires on a Fulbright fellowship and needed someone to take over as visiting fellow in a new "access to justice" program, creating a *pro bono* culture amongst various institutions in the city. We'd had plenty of conversations about work, and he knew how drained I was at the firm. "Monick," he asked, "How would you like to work in Argentina for a year?"

"No way!" I thought. "I can't leave everything I've been working for! It would be nice to do work I could feel passionate about, but I've invested so much getting to this point." I thanked him for thinking of me and hung up the phone. I couldn't just step off the path I'd been on so long. Could I? My stomach grumbled.

I went to my desk and pulled out my passport. It was so full of stamps that I'd had to get extra pages. I was flooded with memories of my beloved travels as I thumbed through the passport pages. I studied my picture on the Japanese visa I had gotten for my semester at Kyushu University, the visa for my post-bar trip to Vietnam, stamps from South Africa where I had spent a summer working with a public interest law firm, stamps from my three months in Paris, where I had gone after college to study French.

My deep love of travel was evident in those pages and pages of stamps. There were dozens of stamps from countries around the world. None from South America, though, I noted. Memories of my overwhelming relief in the hospital mingled with visions of tango halls and colorful nighttime streets. I got on the Internet and checked: I had enough frequent flyer miles for a ticket to Buenos Aires. It was decided.

I was leaving a path on which I had invested nineteen years of school and over five thousand hours as an associate to make partner. The abuse I'd accepted in order to advance was immeasurable. Now I was going to do the most reckless and spontaneous thing

---

*Almost dying was the greatest thing
that ever happened to me.*

I'd ever done and make a leap into an unknown adventure. I felt a little guilty saying farewell to my associate friends at my goodbye lunch; so many were wilting with envy, feeling powerless to unhook themselves from the rat race, while I was so thrilled I couldn't stop grinning. Almost dying was the greatest thing that ever happened to me.

Settled comfortably in seat 24B, I heard the pilot's voice crackle over the loudspeaker, calm and cheerful. "Good morning, ladies and gentlemen. Welcome aboard Flight 209 to Buenos Aires. We have clear skies ahead of us, so expect a flight time of fifteen hours." Clear skies. Anything could happen. *Anything.*

The plane taxied down the runway, and I thought, I'm really doing it. I'm on the plane. And guess what? My stomach doesn't hurt at all.

Monick Halm began her professional life as a corporate litigator in large international law firms before becoming a certified mediator and professional career and life coach. In her "What Am I Going to Do When I Grow Up?" coaching program, Monick helps lawyers and other professionals transition into new careers that are the best fit for them. She is the author of The Inner Game—5 Fun and Daily Habits for Creating Your Ideal Life Balance in 30 Days or Less. *She is also a Reiki Master, painter, writer, yoga practitioner, endurance runner, avid world traveler, wife and mother of three. She focuses on balance and experiencing life as fully as she can and helping clients to do the same. Connect with Monick at www.Equilawbrium.com.*

Justine Arian

Swimming Lessons

A few hours after dark, I feel a tightening and cramping in my belly. And then a wild surge of power moves through my body. The contractions come in waves, wracking me from head to foot. Each one hurls me, crying, against the solidity and comfort of my own mother. The midwives, who have stayed on the phone with John and me through my first throes, rush over as the waves increase in frequency and power. But in the wee hours of the morning, after what feels like an eternity, I'm still only dilated to four centimeters. I'm exhausted, defeated. The pain is unbearable. And I feel totally out of control of what's happening.

My baby isn't budging, no matter what we try. The midwives walk me up and down the street, where I throw up in front of the fire station on the corner. With mounting intensity, one on top of the next, contractions slam me against a wall. I am terrified. What if I don't have the strength to keep doing this? How will I continue to handle this pain? At the peak of a contraction, I even bite John. One of the midwives announces, "If the baby doesn't come down soon, you'll have to go to the hospital."

I snap to from the cloudy fog of labor. "Hell, no!" That would mean handing over control, my biggest fear. A C-section is *not* how my baby is supposed to be born. Determined to take back this experience, I feel adrenaline rushing through my body, and with a gentle push my baby drops into the birth canal. I can feel the change instantly. Within an hour, I'm fully dilated. Now, it's really time to push. The pushing is almost worse than the contractions. I don't know how to handle them both at the same time. Feeling totally out of control, I start to panic. I've prepared myself, body and mind, with yoga, Bradley classes, hypnosis, every book on natural birth I could get my hands on—why can't I handle this?

I'm exhausted, defeated. The pain is unbearable. And I feel totally out of control of what's happening.

"I can't do this!" I scream. "It hurts!" One of the midwives gets right in my face and says, "Yes, you can do it. But you have to trust that you can. Focus, Justine." The midwife has no idea what she is asking me to do. Trust, in a situation I cannot control?

Another contraction racks my body, hurtling me into a memory: I am at the river, with my family. I must be about three years old. It's after lunch, and the afternoon sun sparkles on the water. Everyone is playing, laughing. I'm afraid to enter the water—I can't swim. But my dad holds me tightly in his arms. "It's okay, Justine," he says. "I've got you. I won't let you go. Just give it a try!" I nod, clenching his arms with my small hands and keeping my trembling body pressed as close to his warmth as I can as he wades slowly into the river.

Suddenly, he slips and loses his footing, and I am ejected into the water. It happens so fast—one moment I am safe in his arms, the next I am submerged, panicking, sinking to the bottom of the riverbed. I am totally out of control, flailing my arms and legs in panic, inhaling burning, stinging water through my nose and mouth as I gasp for breath. I have never thought about death before, but I recognize what it feels like. I am drowning, now, and I am going to die. It is only a few seconds before my father reaches me and pulls me, choking, up and out of the water, but it feels like forever. He soothes me, bringing me back to shore. I am held and kissed and dried off, but I can't be comforted. In that moment I realized the only way I could stay safe was to maintain control—always.

It was not until I was in the throes of labor that I felt so out of control and defeated again and realized that, since that day at the river, I had never put myself in a position where it was likely I might be at risk or lose control. During the thirty or so years in between, I did not seek out adventures but stuck to situations I knew I could handle.

For fear of failure, I lacked the confidence to take any risks; I replayed the internal dialogue that I was not good enough. I was the cross-eyed girl, not the pretty one, and, unlike my brother Sean, certainly not smart enough to survive if I went out on a limb. I avoided navigating unknown waters, and any time an exciting but risky opportunity came my way, the same thoughts ran through

---

I did not realize that I lived according to this old self-image—and the fear that if I lost control, I would die.

---

my head: *Justine, you can play around the edge of possibility, but don't go in too deep, you could really drown this time.* I did not realize that I lived according to this old self-image—and the fear that if I lost control, I would die.

When I unexpectedly found out I was pregnant, that old self-doubt and fear rose up with a new intensity. I was excited, yet totally scared of childbirth. I'd come to believe that it was painful, difficult and dangerous—something to be managed, and to survive at best. I didn't imagine it as a potentially empowering experience. Something told me that the cultural norm wasn't the way for me, but I wasn't sure what was. I'd heard of home birth but was uncomfortable with the idea of it. In fact, when my friend spoke of hers, I actually said, "I will never have a home birth!"

What if the pain was too much for me? What if the situation got out of control and something went wrong? Fortunately for me, I grew up in a family that asked a lot of questions, so it was natural for me to ask myself, "What do I want? What are my options? What is a better way to experience birth? The way to keep a handle on this," I thought, "is to be totally prepared, ALWAYS stay in control."

So I set out on a mission to fully educate myself. The part of me that sought validation thought: "I have to do it this way to prove that I am smart, like Sean." So I read everything I could get my hands on, and went to workshops and classes. I met with numerous doctors and midwives. I visited all the hospitals and birthing centers in my area, trying to find the right place to birth my child and the right provider to attend her birth.

After investigating hospitals and finding them sterile, cramped and impersonal, and after visiting birth centers that either emulated doctor's offices or were unable to tell me which midwife would attend the birth of my child, I exhausted my options. The only one left was a home birth. I panicked for a moment. Had I completely lost my mind? My stomach flip-flopped. Was it safe? What if I couldn't handle the pain? What if something went wrong? I'd said *never*. Second thoughts ran through my head. "Who do you think you are, to believe you can have a home birth?" But with support from John and my family, I chose it.

I'd never had a strong sense of self before. But now, for the first time, I began to listen to and trust my inner knowing. Even though it felt like the right choice, I still knew I needed more preparation to feel one-hundred-percent confident with a home birth. The more I prepared and listened to my body, the surer I felt and the more connected I felt to my baby. The decisions I made were coming from that fierce and nurturing mama I had already become, and also from a newfound sense of self I was gaining through this process.

My chosen path also reinforced my need to feel a sense of control over my birthing experience. I felt that by educating myself and choosing my birthing place and team, I would be in control. Little did I know what I would face on that day; it was a rude yet profound awakening.

Coming out of my memory of losing control in the river, I see I have been fighting and resisting this birth, flailing and kicking and choking as if I were drowning. This is the moment of truth. The midwife leans in and insists I focus. I pull myself together—now knowing what I must do. "Relax, Justine, let go and you will float," I tell myself. It takes all my strength and determination, but I force myself to breathe deeply and surrender, giving up my illusions of control.

Instantly, I feel an inner peace and calm pervade my body. "Okay," I exhale, looking my midwife in the eyes. "I *can* do it." Through the intense discomfort, the words bring a smile to my face. And in this moment, I make a choice to overcome a lifetime's worth of fear, distrust and self-doubt held tight. I choose to free myself. Within minutes, my daughter is born.

When they place her on my belly, I blurt, "Oh my God, I have a baby! What do I do now?" High on that cocktail of love hormones that surges through the body right after birth, I realize now that though I'd spent so much time preparing to give birth, I feel totally

> *I know something has transformed in me. Almost as soon as the fear and self-doubt come up, a newfound trust frees me from worry about the journey that lies ahead.*

unprepared as a parent. The midwife just smiles and says, "You love her. You hug her. You kiss her." I hold Jadyn in my arms, hardly able to believe that this beautiful little being has just come out of me. Her eyes are a clear, forget-me-not blue. What ecstasy! How miraculous! We've done it! I fall instantly and completely in love.

I know something has transformed in me. Almost as soon as the fear and self-doubt come up, a newfound trust frees me from worry about the journey that lies ahead. In giving birth to my daughter, I have learned to let go—I have learned how to swim. I look down into Jadyn's beautiful blue eyes and feel so grateful, so powerful. "We did it!" I whisper to her. "You and me, together. We knew how—of course we did. We have everything we need inside of us. Thanks to you, I've discovered my purpose: to help women experience birth and motherhood in a powerful and positive way."

Tears roll down my face as I cradle my daughter's wondrous, tiny body. "You are perfect, just as you are," I tell her and in that moment I understand the power that I seek is not in the control that I attempt to maintain; the true power is in the surrender that I am willing to experience.

Justine Arian, a professionally trained life coach through The Coaches Training Institute (CTI), specializes in individual and group coaching and trainings for mamas and pregnant women, empowering them to claim their inner power and reach their full potential through birth, as mamas and in life, and educating them to make the best choices—from the heart—for themselves and their families. Justine is a certified birth doula (DONA), an independent childbirth educator and a former Bradley® teacher. She is also an RTA-trained personal renewal group facilitator and a certified personal brand strategist. She holds a degree in psychology and social behavior from UC Irvine and works as a marine clerk at the port. Justine lives in Southern California with her partner, John, and their two young children, both born naturally at home. Connect with Justine at www.ThePregnancyCoach.com and www.TheMamaCoach.com.

Mary Parrish

Shades of Grey

I n Afghanistan, the dark is complete.

At two a.m. I'm on my way back from the bathroom, a kind of boxcar near the building that houses my sleeping quarters on the Army FOB (Forward Operating Base). I can barely see my hand in front of my face. There's no structure, nothing—just blackness. I disappear in the long shadows between the lights.

I turn the corner, not ten feet away from my room, and someone grabs my arm, twisting it behind my back. I scream and he yanks harder, forcing me forward as he slams my head into the concrete barrier. His arms are around my throat, choking me. After that, I remember nothing.

When I woke up, my eyes were burning and I could barely see— just enough to tell it was already daylight. I lay inside the concrete barrier, on a pile of rocks. My back felt like it had been run over by a truck. There was a terrible pain between my legs, and my pants were gone. As I struggled to get up, my heart pounded in fear. Where was he now? My head throbbed with pain so excruciating it felt like I had been hit with a bat. I struggled to make it to my room, dizzy and sobbing in fear and disbelief. I was desperately trying to figure out what had just happened to me.

I didn't come out of my room to work that day, and for the next few days after that I couldn't leave it, either. Nobody noticed because

I routinely worked outside the office, installing communications equipment throughout the FOB. Or maybe it was because a soldier in another FOB was killed in a "friendly fire" incident around the same time.

The pain was bad, but my terror was worse. I popped ibuprofen and Ambien constantly, for the pain and to reach the unconscious state it put me in—I was sure that if I didn't take those pills, I would never stop crying. I got to the point where I could hardly walk. All I could do was sit and stare, hoping I had taken enough drugs to not

---

I couldn't fully explain what happened. I was afraid I would be blamed for it.

---

quite wake up. I still only remember those days as a blur, but those who saw me said I was distant. I was smoking cigarettes—and I didn't smoke. I must have talked to my husband, Tracey, because he called my chain of command and said, "What's wrong with my wife? There's something going on. What happened?" We had deployed to Afghanistan together only a couple of months before— but to FOBs forty miles apart. If we hadn't deployed together, our duties would have kept us apart for a full three years.

Tracey had been really worried for my safety. He'd heard all the stories of women being raped and attacked on the FOBs. "Don't go out alone at night," he kept cautioning me. And just a couple weeks before, the first sergeant had advised all females to use what we call a "battle buddy," waking up our appointed buddies in the middle of the night to escort us to bathroom. "I have a hard enough time sleeping," I told him. "If I take these pills and then make a big production out of waking up for the bathroom, I'll never get back to sleep."

I couldn't fully explain what happened. I was afraid I would be blamed for it. I hadn't listened to them. And now this had happened. This terrible thing I had no words for and few images of. I just knew Tracey would be angry and blame me. I went to the doctor because the pain became unbearable. I filed a restricted report. "You need a support system," the doctor said. "You have to tell your husband." I could not tell him what had happened. But my behavior told him something was wrong. He called my chain of command and they started the investigation. Tracey wasn't angry with me. He blamed the chain of command that hadn't listened, hadn't noticed something was very wrong.

The Army flew me to another hospital, where I was tested and put on pain and sleeping meds. Then they actually flew me back to my FOB, where I had to wait while they decided whether or not I would be sent back to Fort Hood.

I didn't know who had done this to me. Was it someone I had trusted? Would he attack me again? I could rarely sleep, and when I did the nightmares were vivid.

My fear was the shadow that followed me back to the base, and to Walter Reed, where I was in the hospital for two weeks. There, they diagnosed me with PTSD (Post-Traumatic Stress Disorder) and seizures, which explained the terrifying memory loss. Still, the fear followed me back home on leave and continued after I finally received a medical discharge from the Army. I hated being near men. Anyone could be him. I couldn't go out at night. I couldn't be in a crowd. My husband couldn't touch me.

I was so tired of not sleeping, tired of being afraid, tired of feeling hopeless, that one day I put a gun in my mouth and pulled the trigger. It clicked. No bullet. That day, I realized: *Something's got to give.*

Every day I woke up to the memory, and went to bed hoping not to dream about it again. I embedded the anger, hatred, disappointment and shame deeper and deeper in my mind. Why was everyone out to get me? Why did God allow this to happen to me? I was raised a Christian. Now, everything I believed about God was in question. "God, what did I do wrong, to deserve this?" When my therapist asked me to read *The Secret*, I became livid, cursing God and asking him, "So, you're saying I attracted this?" Desperate, I also asked, "Why *not* me? So many women have been through this, why am *I* so special?"

Many say you're not supposed to question the will of God. But if I'm not questioning God, how do I find answers? How will I know, if I don't ask? Whom do I ask? I questioned God a lot. No answer was clear. The only precise direction I received was to focus

> *Many say you're not supposed to question the will of God. But if I'm not questioning God, how do I find answers? How will I know, if I don't ask? Whom do I ask?*

on the religious principles that clearly made sense to me, like, "do unto others." As I began to study the evolution of beliefs, I began to see the many shades of grey in life, not the black and white I had imagined there to be before this happened to me.

Before the rape, I gave everyone the benefit of the doubt and was friendly. Many times Tracey would say to me, "You're *too* friendly." *Why do I have to be skeptical of everyone I come into contact with?* I thought. *Have we evolved into a world of hatred and mistrust, and all this time I didn't realize it?* I began to contrast life today with life hundreds of years ago. Back then, it was okay to chop off someone's hand if he stole something. Fifty years ago, blacks were not equal to whites. Twenty years ago, physically disciplining kids was the norm, but today all of these things are unacceptable.

Rape is not new to our generation—it has been going on since the beginning of time. Would someone generations ago in my situation even have considered speaking up? Reporting my rape was humiliating. All the questions they asked that I was unable to answer made the journey even more difficult. I was afraid of what people might say, or that they would not even believe me. I worried about everyone on the FOB knowing, and how it would affect my husband. I was embarrassed. How would people look at me now?

In struggling to make the rape make sense, it hit me one day: *No one can answer "why." I have to define my own why.* That's when I started to change. Instead of fearing everyone, I tried to approach people with virgin eyes, the eyes of goodwill. When I met someone new, my stomach churned, my hands became sweaty, and I started to shake. I wanted to run, but I kept pushing myself past my discomforts.

After several failures, I finally pushed through. When I went back to *The Secret* and combined the Law of Attraction with my new focus, I started to feel good again for the first time in many months. I woke up to inspirational music and went to bed meditating, changing my thoughts and focusing on what I want my future to look like. Although I still felt anxious and afraid, and was still experiencing headaches and fatigue, I could finally see the light at the end of the tunnel.

Now, some days are better than others. Some days I can't leave the house—some days I don't think about the attack. I asked my counselor, "How do I know I'm healed from this and don't need to come to therapy?" She answered, "When it doesn't affect your life." Well, that may take forever. It affects my decisions, my mood,

---

Though the dark can be painful and frightening,
it always has something to teach.

---

when I can or can't be touched or go out. After two years, I still have nightmares and sleepless nights. I do go places and meet new people now, but it's a task, not automatic like it used to be. I used to be very spontaneous, but now I have to plan my adventures, so that I have time to mentally prepare.

Learning to be aware but unafraid is a very challenging balance, but I have to view it as an opportunity. It's much easier to isolate myself from the world than it is to live in the world—but I choose to live in it. The rape is a part of me, now, so I have to find a way to live with it. And I have to live my life for ME. What can *I* live with? How can *I* learn? How can *I* be a better person? I have accepted both that I did attract this event into my life, and that it was not my fault. I'm living in shades of grey, accepting the dark and looking for the light. I think healing just happens that way.

Since I was a kid, I was afraid of the dark. But in Afghanistan, I had to train myself to step out into it without fear. Just when I was beginning to feel more at ease, I was attacked. Now I'm back to baby steps, learning to trust and live again, consciously and not on automatic. This experience has opened my eyes to the truth about life: our experience is what makes us unique. How we deal with our experiences affects the rest of our lives and determines our impact on our family, friends, and the world. And though the dark can be painful and frightening, it always has something to teach.

The grey truth that is still hard for me to accept is that we design our lives and our destinies. When I started asking questions, that's what God showed me. How powerful—and unbelievable. Sometimes I just want to turn my head the other way and let things happen by default, so I can have someone else to blame.

We live in shades of grey, still looking for that perfect black and white answer or direction for our lives, still asking the same questions with each passing day: *When will things be different for me? When will my life change?* There is a lesson in every obstacle in life. I have learned to look for the blessings. I learned that I am the creator and designer of my life. Now I understand why it was me.

Mary Parrish's mission is to help empower people to live beyond their shades of grey. She has an MS in information technology management, which she applied in a military career before she was brutally attacked. She is now medically retired from the military and using her experience to reach others—as a life coach, speaker and as author of the forthcoming book Living in Shades of Grey, Life after Trauma. *Connect with Mary at www.Mary-Parrish.com.*

Nin-Aseeya Ra-El and Arvat McClaine, PhD

A Global Impact

The brick building was perfect, just perfect. Imagine our excitement as we pictured our students learning in the newly renovated building, and running carefree on the playground. We were overjoyed when our architect began taking measurements and drawing up blueprints. Now she just had to make certain that everything could be brought up to meet state code for a school. We anxiously awaited her call so that we could begin construction. But our heads began to spin when we heard the amount of money she said it would take to turn the building into our school. There was no way we could afford it; we were crushed. Back to the drawing board. We needed a building—and fast.

Our mission was simple: to provide an educational experience for urban students that inspired them to do more dreaming, thinking, creating and producing while making them aware of the importance of knowledge, community, family, self and the world. We wanted them to learn compassion for humanity and pride in their African-American heritage, and to experience the wider world. That's why we wanted to open the school.

But when we were out there selling people on the idea of the school, we still had no school to sell. At least, no building. After a story about our school ran in the local paper, our phones rang off the hook. Parents were excited, but they still wanted to know,

"Where's the school going to be?" *Good question,* we thought. "We're in the process of finalizing that now," we said. From there on out we just acted on faith.

Soon enough, though, we found it: a beat-up old warehouse in a pretty neglected neighborhood. It was a dirty gray; a lot of the windows were broken; and the weeds around it were taller than the students we planned to enroll. Inside was worse. It was going to take a major overhaul to make it look nice; it was going to take major work just to make it safe.

"School starts in six weeks," I said, feeling unsure that it would be ready in time. "Well then, we'd better get busy!" Arvat said.

So we went at the building as if we could finish it in time. Panic was a pretty good motivator, too. We were making a lot of promises to a lot of people in our community, and they expected us to deliver. We were exhausted at the end of each day, not only from trying to get everything ready, but also from trying to convince everyone, and sometimes ourselves, that everything would work out.

The first student walked through the door, and the smiles on his and his mother's faces immediately made all of our work worthwhile. We waited for other students to arrive. And waited. And waited. But by the time school had begun, only seven students—that's right, seven—were there.

We needed to furnish our school and a nearby county had an auction of leftover public school supplies. We walked all over a huge hangar but found nothing of use. "Can nothing come easily?" I said to Arvat as we stood in the hangar, unsure whether to laugh or cry. One older gentleman there kept following us. He asked, "What are you two looking for?" We told him, and he smiled. "I'm opening up a fish market in a building I just bought," he said. "It used to be a preschool, and it's got everything you need. Come take all of it for free." *Act as if.* It was as if for every obstacle we encountered, a solution was right around the corner.

We transformed our warehouse, painting the halls in pleasant, calming colors; and we painted each classroom with a different, more stimulating color. We put rocking chairs in the K-2 classrooms. In the halls, we hung portraits of leaders, some well known, some not, with labels explaining who they were. "You can walk through our school and learn without speaking to anyone," we told parents and friends.

We finished our building. We made our entry hall look like a living room, with mauve walls hung with African art and other art from around the world. We also played music there from

---

In order to succeed, our students had to see an example of what success looked like. We were that example. The obstacles that made establishing our school so difficult were a blessing.

---

around the world. Our hall was where we all stood—teachers and administrators—on September 10, 2001, the day we opened. Bristling with excitement, we couldn't wait for the students to arrive. We kept checking our watches.

The first student walked through the door, and the smiles on his and his mother's faces immediately made all of our work worthwhile. We waited for other students to arrive. And waited. And waited. But by the time school had begun, only seven students—that's right, seven—were there. We had had no idea how many students to expect, but we did expect more than seven. We'd received payment for only a few students, but we'd received so many phone calls and applications.

"Who cares?" we said. "Let's make this a great day." And we did. The kids loved it because there were just a few kindergarteners, and one student each in all the other classes. They felt incredibly special and cared for.

That evening, we went out knocking on doors. "Your child missed school today. Why?" Bottom line was the bottom line: "We just don't have the money," parents said. "Don't worry about the money," we said. "Send your kids and we'll figure something out." By the end of that first year, we had thirty-four students.

We worked constantly on widening their perspectives, building their self-esteem and teaching them that the impossible was possible. We taught five languages—Arabic, Chinese, Swahili, Spanish and French. People from other cultures visited to tell about their backgrounds and lives. We had college students come and mentor. Within the school, older children helped to teach the younger children. We had a room where we gathered daily as a community to sing, dance, drum, affirm and celebrate. At meals, the children set the tables and helped clean.

Most of our kids had hardly ever traveled outside of their Richmond neighborhoods. So, it was important to help our kids to expand their vision of the world around them and even more important to help them to believe in themselves. We did everything we knew to achieve those goals. We provided a loving family environment; we had a male and female instructor in each room; and we offered a unique curriculum. And something was working, because at the end of the day, the kids cried when they had to leave. "But are the kids really getting what we want them to get?" we asked. We didn't know. The effects of education are so long-term that you really do have to wait years to measure its impacts.

One mother brought her son to our school because he was failing every class in public school. "I don't know what you can do with my child," she said, in tears. "I have tried everything." "We'll try everything, too," we told her. We were nervous about this one. Sure, we were making kids feel great about themselves, but could we make them better students? With the kids who wanted to be there, we knew we could, but this kid plainly did not want to be there. He sulked when he entered school on his first day. We showered him with warm hellos, but he flat-out ignored them. When his mother put her hand on his shoulder to say good-bye, he angrily shrugged it off.

Every morning, to begin, we gathered in a circle to affirm what we wanted from the day. Some kids said they wanted to get better at math; one child said he wanted to write a really good story. Another said she wanted to draw a beautiful picture of her mother. Our youngest student said he wanted to hear a really good joke, and we all laughed—but not our new kid. His face was set like stone, so glum it was hard not to laugh.

In the afternoon, we gathered again to tell how the day went. Students said various things—they had a great lunch; they learned a new word in three different languages; they felt great for doing well on a test. That youngest student said he did hear a good joke and when he told it to us, we all laughed. And even the new student finally smiled. We all cheered, and he started laughing.

Most of our kids had hardly ever traveled outside of their Richmond neighborhoods. So, it was important to help our kids to expand their vision of the world around them and even more important to help them to believe in themselves.

The next day, when his mother brought him back, she shook her head, amazed. "I don't know what happened here yesterday," she said, "but when he came home, he said, 'Mama, I did not know I was smart.'" The woman hugged us, and she started crying, and we couldn't help crying, too. After she left, Arvat said, "Something's working." "But are they getting it?" I asked. That remained the question and that question hung over us for the entire year. It's one thing to make kids feel good for a day, a week, a month—but it's another for them to really learn, really improve, really believe. And if you tell a child he's great but he keeps failing his classes, then he believes he's not great, and he believes you're not telling the truth. Getting the kids to work hard every day, that's a challenge.

So we all worked hard, every day. Our students worked hard, every day. And that new student who'd been failing every class in public school—he had straight A's by the end of the year. We sat in our office, looking at his report card, amazed. And then it dawned on us: these kids were able to succeed because *we* were able to succeed. Every day, to make our school work, we had to overcome countless obstacles. And every day, in order to become good students, our kids had to overcome countless obstacles.

In order to succeed, our students had to see an example of what success looked like. We were that example. The obstacles that made establishing our school so difficult were a blessing. Over the years, we have seen our students excel and step out of everyday norms. Though most of our previous students have not yet graduated high school, they are taking on amazing projects. They are training to be pilots, recording music, writing and contributing to books and becoming student leaders in the Green Movement. "Wow," we said, "they get it. They really do get it." Yeah. They really did get it. And so did we.

Nin-Aseeya Ra-El is the co-founder of Nubian Village Academy, Inc., the first African-centered school in the state of Virginia. She is currently Executive Director of the school. Aseeya earned a BA in political science with a double minor in philosophy and criminal justice and an MEd in guidance and counseling with a concentration in community counseling, and is working toward her doctorate in metaphysical science. She has served on many community boards in Richmond, VA, and is currently a city commissioner.

Arvat McClaine, PhD, is the co-founder of Nubian Village Academy and currently serves on its Board of Directors. She recently authored a book in conjunction with the Nubian Village Academy community entitled Amazing Faces of Central Virginia. *Along with her husband Harold Watkins, Dr. McClaine has operated several successful businesses that have nurtured the minds and spirits of many. She holds a doctorate in parapsychic science and has completed all of the coursework for a doctorate in urban education. To connect with Aseeya and Arvat, visit www.NubianVillageAcademy.com.*

Hilde Vercaigne

Welcome Back

To my mother, brother and sister, my father had two faces: sober and angry, or drunk and violent. To me, his favorite, his "smart girl," his spitting image, he showed a third, secret one.

I hated being alone with my father, but because he didn't mind "babysitting" me—three kids were too many for him to handle— my mother always left me alone with him. To make sure he came right home from his own outings, instead of going out drinking, she sent me along. My mother was so happy he was paying attention to *one* of his children that when he wanted to shower with me, she did not object. After all, he loved me. I was the sacrifice necessary to maintain equilibrium in my family.

The severe asthma attacks started when I was about three. When I was five, I was placed in a sanatorium for sick children for a short time and got better almost immediately. Everyone was amazed at my recovery. But once I got home, I was sick with severe asthma again. A few years later, after a whole year at another children's sanatorium, I returned healthy to Belgium only to become sicker than ever a short while later. My father was always angry with me for being sick. It meant I was bad, he said. It was a sign of weakness. I was only his favorite when I was healthy and could be of some use to him. And he was angry with my mother for taking care of me when I was sick.

When my father was drunk, he hit my mother, pushed her, screamed at her. But he told me he would never do that to me if I were nice to him. I knew this meant my allowing him to continue to touch me. When he did, I felt terribly, darkly guilty getting the love my mother should have gotten from him. Drunk, he crashed his car again and again, but miraculously, he rarely got hurt, and then never seriously. I felt guilty for wishing something would happen to him; but I cried and felt sorry for him if he did suffer.

To make myself less attractive to my father, I became a tomboy. I wore my brother's old clothes, got my hair cut super-short and made sure I was always dirty from playing outside. It didn't help. He treated me like I was his lover because I was "special." "You're

---

I was the sacrifice necessary to maintain equilibrium in my family.

---

just like me," he said, and I hated myself for that because I hated my father. Because I looked like him, I couldn't stand seeing my face in the mirror. In every family photo, I am either grimacing or turned deliberately away from the camera.

One Sunday afternoon when I was about ten, while I was walking with my parents in the woods near our house, my father held me back as my mother moved ahead of us. She became a speck. He looked at me with an intense, passionate expression and kissed me. Horrified, I screamed and tried to push him away, but he held his hand over my mouth and warned me not to make a sound.

The look in his eyes terrified me. It was worse than the empty expression he sometimes wore when he touched me, as if he was erasing us both. I was his outlet, and that kept the others safe. Otherwise, my mother might not have survived.

Since that terrifying day in the woods, I never wanted to sit in his lap anymore, or be alone with him. My mother didn't understand the change in my behavior. "Be nice to your father,

Hilde," she would say. "Don't make him angry. Behave." I was too afraid to tell her what was really going on when my father and I were alone, for fear that she might say something to him and die as a result, or worse, that she would tell me not to make waves. In a house full of people, I felt so alone.

At twelve, I was overjoyed to go to boarding school all week long.

---

*But still, I felt guilty. I knew my saying
no meant endangering my family.*

I made a friend there, whose scouting troop I joined. I escaped to her house at least every other weekend. Her family was kind, loving in the right way, and they embraced me warmly. The contrast with my own family was so great I could hardly believe these people were real. It finally dawned on me: This is how a family is *supposed* to be.

When I came home, I had changed. I started standing up for myself. The first time he tried to touch me again, before I knew it, I heard myself saying, "NO!" To my surprise, I found myself feeling more angry than scared. He knew that his days of being my unwanted lover were over, so from that time forward, all my father and I ever did was fight. He called me ugly, saying that no man would ever want me: I was "used material." When I came in at the top of my class, his response was, "You're just lucky the rest of your class is even more stupid than you are." He became a bigger threat to everyone, wildly violent, unpredictable and an even worse drinker. I stayed away more than ever, hoping that he would be calmer if he did not see me.

But still, I felt guilty. I knew my saying no meant endangering my family. I was the reason for my father's bad behavior: the estranged, angry girl who turned her back on her family every chance she got. By the time I was nineteen and working in my parents' business, the harassment from my father was worse than ever and my mother's blame was constant, total. "What did you do this time?" she would yell at me, every time he lost control.

One morning, still fuming about the latest argument with my mother—"You used to be his favorite!"—I glower at my dad-like reflection in the driver's side window as I unlock my car and slam myself inside it. As I drive, I think, *Where is the breaking point? I can't stand it anymore.*

All day I walk around dead but upright, feeling like all my guts have been sucked out, leaving my insides empty. And I wake up sick to my stomach every morning. If someone would say to me, "You will die in fifteen minutes," I will believe it. Why do I even get up?

My mother sends me to a shrink to try and fix me, so I don't upset my father anymore. No one can help me. *Ugly. Stupid. Used material.*

A blast of car and truck horns suddenly jerks the dark, tight knot of my thoughts and, quickly re-focusing on the road, I see a bus coming at me head-on. I'm paralyzed with fear, panicking. My body has frozen up completely. As if directed by a separate mind, my car veers off the road and straight for a house. I manage to make my hands turn the steering wheel, but the rest of me seems to have gone completely numb. I can't find the brakes. I crash straight into the front of the house.

Everything goes dark and totally silent. And then I see myself, lying there on the pavement, people scurrying around me. I don't feel any pain at all, but a strange kind of peace. In this moment—a second, minute, lifetime?—I see a little girl with dark curly hair and dimples in a little white dress, running barefoot across a sunlit field toward a smiling man, who reaches out his hand to her. She gives me the most wonderful smile, and I begin to shake with an overwhelming joy. Then I see that the little girl is me, and the man is my father. I shake so hard my head bounces on the road. A voice says, "Welcome back."

Reality. I hear the wail of sirens, the sound of voices. I try to respond but I can't speak; my mouth is filled with blood and what feels like broken teeth. Strong arms lift me. Soon I wince under bright hospital lights. I am thoroughly examined, injected with tranquilizers and given painkillers. Later—it must be morning— I wake up in a strange room. Sunlight streams through the curtains. A gentle voice speaks, but I cannot make out what it is saying. A nurse stands over me, carefully washing my face with a sponge. "Where am I?" I ask her. "What is happening? Am I all right?" All that comes out is a long moan, and tears.

Everyone handles me with great care, as if I really am someone special. They encourage me, celebrating every milestone with me as I heal. For the first time, surrounded by love, I am grateful to be alive.

The doctor comes in and tells me it is a miracle I've survived the crash. I am a collection of broken bones, including several breaks in my jaw. I have a bad concussion, and innumerable cuts and bruises. "All this will heal, eventually," he tells me, "but it will take at least ten days before we can operate. With your concussion, I'm afraid you could go into a coma if we do it before then." I just have to wait. Cuts are stitched, hundreds of glass shards removed from my body. I start praying, hard, for my recovery. Just let me get well, God, I beg. Just let me be me again.

My father visits after checking out the car: first things first. "It's a total loss," he says, then sits there for a short while in stoic, angry silence. I remember my vision of us and am filled with a warm glow. It feels like the best medicine in the world. And yet the man next to me is not the man in the vision. Will he ever be? Seeing me cry, thinking it is pain or weakness, my father gets up abruptly and leaves.

Several days later, a surgeon comes to tell me about the reconstructive surgery planned for me. He has called in a jaw reconstruction-specialist to perform a new procedure that will minimize major scarring. "We're going to do the best surgery ever seen. I do not want a beautiful young woman to lose her face." *Me? A beautiful young woman? What is he seeing that I am not?*

When I wake up from surgery, my bed has been moved to face the mirror so I can look at myself. I see a classic movie mummy, bandages and tape covering my head and jaw. I know that underneath my bandages will be a new face, forever changed. But two familiar eyes peek out of the costume, full of light I don't remember seeing in them before. The surgeon worries about a lump on my neck, and another possible operation to remove it. I am not worried, not one bit. I'm alive!

The anesthesiologist who had been at the scene of the accident arrives with a special ointment he has made. He says it will reduce the lump over time and possibly even make it disappear. I'm touched; he does not have to be here, is not actually treating me. Nurses gently rub salves and ointments into my lumps, bumps and cuts. My old babysitter, now a nurse in the hospital, comes

---

I may have crashed, but I did not burn.

---

to see me every day. Two boys I knew from the scout troop ride their bikes forty-five minutes each way to visit me. My sister comes and falls asleep on the bed as we talk. The sight of her blond hair streaming across the pillow makes me cry. Everyone handles me with great care, as if I really am someone special. They encourage me, celebrating every milestone with me as I heal. For the first time, surrounded by love, I am grateful to be alive.

When my father comes again to visit, saying nothing, I see him differently. He doesn't frighten or anger me; he is just another soul. Instead of feeling pain for him, I feel myself letting him go, to do what he will. I let go of the man who hurt me. I let go of the fantasy-father in the vision, who will never be. When he leaves, I think, *It's okay if I never see you again.*

I took the fall for my family, first because I was vulnerable, and then because I was strong. I stepped into my mother's shoes to save her, and learned a bitter, terrifying inversion of love; I stepped into my father's shoes and learned to hate myself, feeling I had no choice.

Today as I walk on my own out the hospital's big main doors, I make one decision: *I think now I'll try my own damn shoes on for a while.* I no longer have to hurt at the hands of my father, or for my mother's safety. I may have crashed, but I did not burn. And now it's my turn to lift up my new face and smile a *real* smile. Yes, welcome back, Hilde!

In sharing her story, Hilde Vercaigne hopes to help others see they are not alone, and that every day we are given new chances to be who we most want to be—ourselves. Her life's purpose is to inspire others to courageously walk their own path. Connect with Hilde at www.HildeVercaigne.com.

Lisa Shultz

An Unlikely Gift

We sat in the living room, watching a movie, a comedy. Our two daughters were in bed, I was on the couch, and my husband was in "his chair." I don't remember what movie it was, but I do remember it was funny. Yet I wasn't laughing. "I used to laugh at this stuff," I thought to myself that night. But I felt beaten down, and I couldn't laugh anymore, at anything.

For much of my life, if there had been an award for laughing, I would have won it. As a child, I was nicknamed "The Laughing Hyena." Every two weeks in the third grade, the teacher moved my desk, thinking I wouldn't laugh as much next to different kids. Never worked, not even when she moved my desk near hers.

When my husband and I started dating, he loved to create nicknames for me and other people. His favorite for me was "darling." Most of his friends didn't know my real name and always said, "Hi, darling!" He always made me laugh at his wit and playfulness. Little did I know that ten years after we got married, "darling" would be replaced by words like "bitch."

The first time I saw a shift in his personality was about three years into our marriage. We had adopted a dog from the Humane Society and named her Sally. We came home one night after being out, and Sally, still just a puppy, had chewed up our doormat. This was annoying, but hardly a big deal. My husband didn't agree. For the first time, he went into a rage. "You bad dog," he yelled, with alarming venom. He smacked Sally with an open hand. She crouched in shock and fear, and he smacked her again, hard. He then picked up the doormat and started hitting Sally with it, repeatedly. Sally yelped and cowered in a corner but couldn't get away. Baffled and scared, I shouted, "Stop it!" He continued to beat Sally. I ran to him and put my arms around him to pull him away.

He was big and solid, but somehow I pulled him away. "What are you doing?" I asked, breathless. His face red, he shouted, "She deserves it, Lisa!" At that moment, I knew that something

> *Little did I know that ten years after we got married, "darling" would be replaced by words like "bitch."*

in him, in us, had changed. This was my first real glimpse of his emerging narcissism. A typical tactic of narcissists is to blame their victims for their own rage. For the narcissist, nothing is ever his fault, and he can never be wrong.

Once the dust settled from that incident, I made it very clear to my husband how unacceptable his behavior had been. And he never did something like that again—to Sally. Instead, he focused most of his rage on others, and then the person closest to him—me. So much of it was about completely trivial issues.

One afternoon I came home from the hair salon. "Your hair looks like shit," he said. He got so angry I had to beg him not to go to the salon and accost the beautician. Another morning, I brought him pancakes. "Why is it so hard for you to make these round?" He criticized me more and more, and his words got progressively more degrading. "You stupid cunt." Yep. He said it. The "C" word that every woman dreads.

Rage goes hand in hand with narcissism. He saw a strong woman and then tried to beat her down. When he had the power to deflate, degrade and demoralize someone else, he felt superior and better about himself. So I pulled completely within myself. I tiptoed around the house, scared of triggering his rage. It was hard to look my best, because often he told me I was fat or wearing my clothes the wrong way. My confidence in my physical appearance shrank, as did my overall self-esteem. I slowly realized that he was murdering my soul.

I also stopped asking him for any kind of help around the house. Every time I had, he always said no, and that constant refusal just wore me down. One New Year's Eve I sat in my room, writing out my resolutions for the year. I wrote, "Never ask for

---

I was the frog, and the pot of my life had been growing hot for years.

---

anything from him." My life was such a misery—and it had all happened so slowly I hadn't even noticed. It wasn't until that night when we were watching a comedy and I couldn't laugh that I realized how far down I'd gone, with no inner resources to pull myself up. It was like the famous illustration of the frog in boiling water. Put it in a boiling pot, and it leaps out; but put it in a pot of cool water and let the water slowly warm, and the frog doesn't know that it's dying until it's too late for it to save itself. I was the frog, and the pot of my life had been growing hot for years.

At Christmas in 1998, we hosted a ton of family members. I had a terrible cold, but still did everything—cooked, cleaned, shopped, wrapped the presents. At Christmas dinner, I asked him to pour the wine, and he said, "No." A couple of days later, it snowed heavily. I came into the living room where he sat reading the paper. I asked if he could go out and shovel. We had a large driveway and a lot of sidewalks. Again, he refused. Shoveling outside in the cold, tears freezing on my cheeks, I wondered how he had gone from doting on me and showering me with gifts and affection to offering only indifference, cruelty and spite.

The following week, he said, "I need to tell you something." I nodded, my head stuffed. "I've been having an affair." That sledgehammer hit came fast, knocking out the little wind left in my body. I wasn't sure if the congestion in my head made me hear absurd things, or if the man I loved had just confessed to an affair. Another, larger, body blow was coming my way in his next sentence. "You and I are getting a divorce, and I'm going to marry her. That's what's happening, and don't even think about asking me to change my mind." Crushed under the pressure from these blows to my heart and the illness in my body, I was dismissed.

That next month was the absolute worst of my life. Every day, I woke up, got the girls off to school, and returned to bed, where I hid under the blankets and sobbed. In the evening, I'd make dinner, then go to bed and sob some more, claiming I still didn't feel well from my cold. I sobbed so much that if I had to take the girls to a music lesson or some other function, I wore sunglasses, even inside, to hide my swollen, red eyes.

And that's when it hit me: that woman, the one he left me for, was a gift: her presence in his life was the hand that reached into the pot of hot water and pulled me out.

By the end of January 1999, I was finished sobbing. I still felt devastated, but I thought about my daughters. For their own health and their own futures, they needed to see a strong mother. They needed me to get out of the pot of boiling water. First, I got an attorney. We went to court in April, and after hearing the facts, the judge immediately said to my husband, "You've got three days to get out of the house." Up to that point, he had refused to move out despite the fact that he was openly having an affair.

One day, I tracked down the woman he was going to marry. I had a picture of the four of us—me, my husband and our two daughters. I handed her the picture and said, "How can you destroy us?" I was so angry with her for what I perceived were her intentions to steal my husband away from me and shatter our family.

Though life with him was miserable, I still fought the idea of a divorce. My own parents had divorced, and it was rough for me. I'd sworn I would never get a divorce. During the separation, I joined a divorce support group. The group had a specific, nine-week program, and that helped, but just as valuable was when the group got together for social activities. We went to dances, movies, restaurants. It helped to be surrounded by people who, like me, were all trying to regain their lives. We laughed. A lot. I got laughter back into my life pretty quickly just by being separated from my husband.

Until I was free of the oppression I had endured, I did not realize that it had been like carrying around a bag of potatoes on my shoulders. Once he left the house, I found myself surrounded by supportive family and friends both old and new. I put down the sack of potatoes and stood up straight. When I looked in the mirror, I was again able to see the beauty I'd always had, but had forgotten under his litany of criticism.

At first, I was almost shocked when a man told me how beautiful I was; it had been so long since I had heard loving and nurturing words. Each time someone gave me the gift of a kind word or compliment, I let it soak in like water to a withering plant. That sad plant gradually stood up straight and showed healthy leaves. With more time, space and loving water showered on me by others, I even bloomed again.

I also started seeing a therapist during my recovery. In our first session, after I told her about everything—his affair and his treatment of me—she said, "That woman was a gift to you." I responded, "Are you kidding? She destroyed me, my family, and my life." My therapist let me vent before she repeated, "No, she didn't destroy your life. She saved it. She was a gift." It took me years to understand that. I simply wasn't able to see a silver lining wrapped up in an experience I felt so much anger about. But with time, I got it, realizing that I was like that frog boiling to death in my own marriage.

And that's when it hit me: that woman, the one he left me for, was a gift: her presence in his life was the hand that reached into the pot of hot water and pulled me out. His leaving me wasn't what I thought a gift would look like, which is why it took so long for me to recognize it. Today, I am a fully-realized woman with a successful business. And I have joy and laughter. My daughters are full of life, and because they witnessed my determination to find my way back to happiness, they know how to find—and keep—joy and laughter in their own lives. And to think: I would not be the powerful woman I am today without my unlikely gift.

Lisa Shultz is the owner and founder of Women, Wine & Wellness, a networking organization focused on connecting and empowering women. She is an expert on the art of networking and business success strategies, and through her work as an author and speaker Lisa has touched thousands of lives. Her lifelong passion for learning and helping others led her to her heart's work: inspiring women to speak their truth and supporting them in sharing their personal stories. Lisa co-created the book Speaking Your Truth: Courageous Stories from Inspiring Women *and co-authored the book* How to Bring Your Book to Life This Year. *Learn more about her books at www.SelfPublishingExperts.com. She lives in Denver, Colorado, with her two daughters. Connect with Lisa at www.LisaShultz.com.*

Brent Phillips

A Modern Wizard

Pancakes. Twenty-eight years old and your mom's cutting your pancakes. It was bad enough when she did the sausage, but at least that's gristly. And she's been cutting your meat ever since you moved home two years ago, so you're used to that. But pancakes? "You don't have to do that, Mom," I tell her. "It's no big deal," she says. "Yeah, it is," I say, feeling totally useless and dependent, wondering if things can get any worse, wondering how I can possibly repay her.

Three years before, I was living my dream as the Chief Technical Officer of two successful Internet companies. I had always been fascinated by magic and miracles; I'd grown up playing *Dungeons & Dragons,* reading tons of science fiction, fantasy and mythology and wishing to be a wizard! But I thought magic and miracles only happened in stories, movies, or thousands of years in the past—so instead I became a wizard of technology. And I poured my heart and soul into the role.

My life plan was to make a ton of money from my Internet companies and then devote myself to mystical and spiritual pursuits. But as the lead programmer and software architect for two companies, I was regularly working close to one-hundred hours per week. A year and a half of that schedule took its toll. By the time I was twenty-six, my body had completely broken down.

The worst pain was in my elbows and wrists, where my nerve endings felt like they were being twisted with a pliers. My shoulders, neck and back all felt like I had just been through twelve grueling rounds of Mike Tyson pounding my body to a pulp. Months passed, the pain increased, and doctors put me on more medications. They prescribed all forms of physical therapy. Nothing worked. *How can this be? I am so young. There must be a different medication I can take. There must be some regimen that can fix this.*

Then one day, the bomb dropped. My primary physician declared me "permanent and stationary." "What does that mean?" I asked. He said, "It means you'll never be able to work again, and all we can do is try to help manage your pain." He paused before he delivered the final blow, then added, "Recovery is impossible." When a world-class orthopedic surgeon says, "You'll never recover,"

---

*By the time I was twenty-six, my body
had completely broken down.*

---

you tend to believe him, and I did. Depressed and confused, I moved back into my parents' house and took the spare room. Soon I was in too much pain to work, so I lost my position and went on disability. Then my partners went behind my back and promptly sold for millions of dollars the company I had crippled myself to build.

I tried to play video games, but the pain was too severe. I couldn't read because I couldn't hold a book open. I could drive, but no more than ten minutes at a time. A liquor store was within that range, so my days were filled with the three Ds: drinking, drugs and depression. In between, Mom cut my food. I couldn't imagine things getting any worse: I had lost my companies; was forced to live with my parents; was told I could never work again; and, at twenty-six, was crippled and in constant pain with no hope of recovery. Drunk or high, the load lightened a bit, but when I was sober, I felt every kind of pain. "I need a miracle," I told myself, sucking on another bottle of booze. "I need a wizard." But then I remembered: wizards aren't real, and miracles stopped happening thousands of years ago.

One day, my mom drove me to my massage therapist. It was a gorgeous spring day—trees budding, flowers blooming, sunshine bright. As Mom drove, I thought, "I'm so pathetic I can't even enjoy this day." She stopped the car near the front entrance, and I shuffled painfully inside for my weekly massage.

At the end of my treatment, my massage therapist said, "Have you ever considered alternative medicine, Brent?" I shrugged. I was vaguely aware of things like acupuncture, but I wasn't entirely sure what "alternative medicine" entailed. "No," I said, "but I'm

---

"I need a miracle," I told myself, sucking on another bottle of booze. "I need a wizard." But then I remembered: wizards aren't real, and miracles stopped happening thousands of years ago.

---

willing to try anything." A glimmer of hope quickly turned me into a full-time patient! I went to acupuncturists and herbologists and all sorts of healers and bodyworkers; I did yoga, body cleanses, Tai Chi and Nei Kung; and I tried tons of different supplements, healing machines and a strict raw food diet. You name it, I did it. And yet I still just slowly got worse. My glimmer turned back into depression.

After five years of treatments, my lawyer came by the house. I lay in bed in sweatpants and a T-shirt, too sore to move. He pulled a chair up next to me. I secretly envied his being on the job, his ability to move a chair. "You're near the end of your insurance," he said. "They don't want to pay anymore." I'd spent most of the money I had made from my companies. "What do you recommend?" I asked. "It's risky, but there's an experimental surgery you can try." *No risk can be worse than my life,* I thought. "Let's try it," I said.

I didn't know if I could stand the disappointment again, but as they prepped me for surgery, I found myself wishing for a miracle.

After surgery, my surgeon came to my bedside in the recovery room. "How about moving your arms for me," he said. I bent my left elbow and lifted my hand, but I couldn't move my right arm. I tried a few times and failed. "Well, that's interesting," he said, nonchalant, detached. There was no miracle. I couldn't move my arm, and he didn't care. I did months more physical therapy, but it didn't work.

"There's nothing left," I said to myself one day, as I downed another glass of whiskey. "My only choice is to end it quickly or let this take years." That's when my aunt Lauren called. "I've got someone I want you to meet."

Terry O'Connell was a friend of my aunt Lauren. She worked for the Department of Commerce on steel trade; did corporate finance for oil companies; and had opened her own consulting firm. Then she got terribly ill. No doctor could tell her what was wrong. Desperate, she visited Vianna Stibal, founder of Theta Healing, and in five minutes she had her answer and her cure. Terry's office was a small but sunny, airy room and Terry's pretty face and comforting smile put me at ease. Since her own healing experience, she'd dedicated her life to Theta Healing. Though I didn't know it at the time, I was her first professional client.

She explained the entire process of Theta Healing and showed me how to do muscle testing. Then she asked what I thought about God. "I've always been fascinated by spirituality," I said. "I got my introduction to it through martial arts when I was young. I always planned to pursue mysticism and spirituality, but now I know that's never going to happen." *This conversation is interesting,* I thought, *but I have no idea what it has to do with my arm.*

At the end of our session, she did a healing on me that lasted just a couple of minutes. I actually felt something pop and shift in my elbow, and she told me to go ahead and move it. Doubtful, I went ahead and played along. My miracle had come! I could move my arm freely and easily! "Oh, my God," I said. "I don't know what just happened, but I have to learn this." "Vianna is coming to town in September, and she's giving one of her seminars. You can learn then," Terry smiled. September was three months away; the wait was agony. When the seminar did finally come around, it was another revelation. I committed my life to Theta Healing, which involved a lot of studying and seminars.

At first, Mom was worried I'd joined a cult. One day, just returned from a training session, I took Mom swimming. She'd had polio when she was four and suffered from post-polio syndrome her whole life; her left leg was often swollen and painful. The doctors didn't want to touch her because of the risk of blood

---

I had done thousands of healings by then, and I'd seen so many miracles I'd grown used to them. I expect them. Nonetheless, my mom's was, without a doubt, my most important healing.

---

clots. At the swimming pool, I said, " Can we do a healing session on your leg, Mom?" "Sure," she said. The next day, at breakfast, she was in tears. "What's wrong?" I asked. "Nothing's wrong, Brent. My pain and swelling are pretty much gone." It meant so much to be able to do something for her after all she had done for me.

Mom became a believer and supporter; little did we know how vital that would be in years to come. In January of 2010, Mom sat my sister and me down and told us she'd been diagnosed with clear cell endometrial cancer—a very aggressive cancer with a five-year survival rate of less than five percent. It was a death sentence. My sister sobbed uncontrollably, but I was very calm. *It's going to be okay,* I thought. *Everything is going to be all right.* I understood, now, that even the darkest diagnosis could be temporary.

As we neared Mom's surgery date, I gathered a group of my top students and we did a healing on her. Two weeks after her surgery, the surgeon called with the news. "I have no idea what happened," he said. "When we did the biopsy, clear cells were everywhere, but when we examined the tissue that we removed, all the clear cells were gone." Doctors don't often use the word "miracle," but this sure looked like one. I had done thousands of healings by then, and

I'd seen so many miracles I'd grown used to them. I expect them. Nonetheless, my mom's was, without a doubt, my most important healing.

Years ago, I'd set out to make my millions; retire to some tropical island I'd bought; and split my time between hot-tubbing with supermodels and pursuing the mystical and the spiritual. I did make millions, but then lost it all due to an illness so debilitating that I was reduced to having my mother cut my food. It was that very illness that led me to real-life magic and miracles.

I am ninety percent recovered. And I'm glad it's been a slow recovery, for if it had been too quick, I'm not sure I would have turned my life over to healing others. And had I not done that, I may not have been able to help heal my mother. Her doctor, my doctor and many others are surprised by our recoveries. I'm not.

A scientist, engineer and self-professed computer nerd, Brent Phillips never thought he'd be doing anything like Theta Healing. In 1995, he left his PhD program at MIT to become a founding partner in the Jamison/Gold Interactive Agency, a high-end web design and consulting firm. In 1996, he founded Lyra Studios, the video game developer responsible for the game Underlight. *But a debilitating illness changed his life, and today he is a certified Master of Theta Healing. He is the author of two books about the practice,* Where Science Meets Spirit: The Formula for Miracles *and* Spiritual Weight Loss; *and has developed the groundbreaking Formula for Miracles technology. Connect with Brent at www.ThetaHealingLA.com and www.FormulaForMiracles.net.*

Dr. Karen E. Johnson

Secrets and Lies

The orderlies have just brought me back to my ER room from my hip x-ray, and as I sit looking at all its familiar items (I was an ER nurse before becoming a doctor)—the blood pressure cuff and red hazardous materials container attached to the wall, the box of gloves on the counter—everything seems so sterile, so alone. Like me. What am I doing, back here again? Embarrassment and shame cover me like a veil.

The pain in my hip was severe enough at four o'clock this morning to wake me. I was so worried I finally gave in and drove to the hospital. *Is my hip broken? Why am I still having so much pain?* In my head I could hear him say, "I didn't kick you *that* hard. I didn't even have my shoes on!" *I just want the pain to go away,* I cry softly to myself. *I want my life back.*

The nurse practitioner comes in. "The good news," she says, "is that nothing is broken. The bad news is, I have to report this incident, and your boyfriend, to the police." In the seconds after she speaks, I see my whole life come crashing down. I am going to die if this gets out! "Oh, no—you can't!" I plead with her as I imagine the TV coverage: "Doctor Beats Doctor in Domestic Dispute." "Dr. Karen Johnson, the abused…." I see my son being taunted at school and swim practice. I see my former partners and friends snickering: "She deserved it; I always knew she was weak."

My brand new practice, that I have worked a lifetime to build, will collapse—what will my patients think?

"How can I help them when I can't even help myself?" I think. "Why didn't I leave after the last time?" Still, I beg the nurse not to report the incident. In her eyes, I read the stories I'd once shared around my own hospital: stories of women who were clearly being abused, and would ultimately end up paying for their silence with their own lives. But with great reservation, and even fear for my life, she honors my request—but only because we were not living together.

"Stupid black b___!" he yelled. "Stupid black b___!" I hear him yelling in my head as if he were right here. Edgar was everything I'd ever wanted in a man: "eye candy," good dancer, great in bed, distinguished, educated and successful, a physician like myself. He was so good with Jamaal, who needed a father figure. He was

---

"Stupid black b___!" he yelled. "Stupid black b___!" I hear him yelling in my head as if he were right here.

---

a fabulous cook. He loved to play Scrabble and golf. And such a romantic! We met in the winter; between the end of January and right up to Valentine's Day, he orchestrated a series of love notes so I received one every single day. I was used to being smarter than the men I dated, but he was smarter than me. I looked up to him. I fell harder for him than I'd ever fallen before. I finally had what I'd wanted.

Our first months together were paradise. Edgar knew exactly what to do, and he did it masterfully. And then "we" turned into a nightmare. The perfect relationship had somehow become my big dirty secret. *Stupid black b___!* I never knew what would set him off, but when he lost control, he raged, screaming at me, hitting and kicking me and pushing me to the floor. *Come on, motherf___!* He taunted me as if we were fighting man-to-man. Most of the time he took care to make bruises only where they could be easily covered up, but once he squeezed my temple so hard I thought he'd broken one of the tiny bones in my jaw joints. Fearing a future of excruciating pain on and off, I had to have my jaw checked. I lied at the ER and said, "I think I might have TMJ and need it ruled out."

Another time he bruised my eye and it turned a blazing red. Gary, one of the other partners in our practice, took me aside and said, "Karen, tell me Edgar did not do this to you." I lied and said he hadn't. "The reason I'm asking you this is," he said, "the last woman he dated told me he put his hands on her." My stomach flipped: so there were others. But I wasn't ready to face the truth. I painted on my best professional, stoic face, and replied, "I don't believe a word that woman says." The conversation was closed.

I made up every excuse for Edgar. I should try not to make him so angry—but the anger emerged from nowhere: *I had a dream about this already. I dreamed three times I knocked all your motherf___g teeth out.* Then I thought it was the alcohol. Or maybe it was his marriage—I never got the true story about it, but from what I could patch together she had dumped him. *No wonder he can never, ever tell me he loves me,* I told myself. *He's got a lock on his heart and he can't bring himself to say it because he's so hurt.*

My own heart was breaking after each episode and the marks began to linger. Though they were hidden from public view, when I dressed in front of the mirror, the scratches, welts and bruises never seemed to fade. It was as if my body and spirit were speaking to me: *Don't do this to me again, please!* But I could not listen. My need for him was greater than my love for myself. *I'm just going to have to get love the way he gives it,* I decided. I made him what I wanted him to be. I thought I could fix him with love.

We are both educated. If I could just get him to go to counseling with me, if I could just show him how good he really is, how much he deserves love! Sometimes he really listened, and his apologies and remorse seemed so genuine. So I wrote him poems, trying to appeal to the sensitive, creative side of his nature:

I am one of your ribs/I was not the Best/So don't feel that our relationship must be a contest/I, like you, was made in God's image/An image that should be revered and not abused

We were together for more than five years. Inside, I felt like I was failing myself. I was a master faker. I kept telling myself I was doing it for Jamaal, who had no idea what was happening. Edgar's

> *I was so happy to find somebody powerful and smart for the first time—but then, I felt overpowered. He controlled everything, down to the color of my suits and the amount of makeup I wore.*

sisters, waving a carrot over my head, said, "You're the only one that's lasted this long! I think he's going to marry you!" I *wanted* him to marry me! Logic had been stripped out of me, to the point that I was even willing to say, "I do" to a lifetime of abuse. Where was the powerful woman I used to be? I didn't even recognize myself.

Every time the venom came out—*"Go on, b___, if you're going to leave just get the hell out!"*—the honey was close behind. We had a honeymoon after every violent episode. He'd make a fabulous dinner… we'd go upstairs… he'd have the Jacuzzi running with bubble bath and candles, and he would touch me like he had when we first met. All of that tender love and care was so superficial. I knew exactly what would happen, like clockwork, every time. But I stayed, for every unhealthy reason. I felt incredible guilt and shame for the failure of my marriage because my ex-husband said I had "emasculated him." Edgar was mature and in control; he would never use such a lame excuse! I was so happy to find somebody powerful and smart for the first time—but then, I felt overpowered. He controlled everything, down to the color of my suits and the amount of makeup I wore.

One morning, I asked Edgar why he hadn't invited me to go with him to visit his family. We were all close, I thought, and I had cared for his sister and her husband when they were both seriously ill. "My family doesn't want you around," he snarled. I was flabbergasted. So I called his bluff: "I'm just going to call to see what I did wrong, and make it right." He rushed over, cursing me, and grabbed the phone out of my hand. Then he hurled me against the wall. I painfully picked myself up off the floor and blurted, "It's not worth it, Edgar. I'm not doing this anymore." I had no idea what I had just initiated.

A new rage exploded in Edgar. He pushed me onto his bed, grabbed his handgun and pointed it at me, screaming, "I'm going to blow your motherf__ing head off! And then I'll call Jamaal to tell him about it!" He yanked me off the bed. I fell to the floor. He kicked me and stomped on my left hip. "You're right!" I cried, in pain and terror. "I shouldn't have said anything. Please don't do

---

"Mom, you are a queen," he gently whispered, as we held each other close. "And if a man can't see that in you, he doesn't deserve you." I wept and wept: my child had to tell me what I should have known all along.

---

this!" He *would* kill me. I could see it in his face—the man I loved wasn't even in there. I'd known about the gun. *Why didn't I see this coming?* I pictured Jamaal, alone without a father *or* mother. I saw him identifying my body at a morgue. That pain was more grueling than the beating.

Then the phone rang, and my heart jumped. I was amazed when Edgar went to answer it. While he was distracted, I ran for the door. He yelled after me as I limped away from his house and tore out of the driveway, but he didn't follow. I couldn't believe I'd escaped.

It was about a week after the attack when I found myself in the ER, hoping he hadn't broken my hip, and that the truth would not come out. I needed prayers. I needed help. I needed to find my own lost strength again. I had been so close to losing my life.

Even though my spirit was wounded, it was not completely broken. Finally, I found the courage to leave.

After many hours of counseling, tears, peeling off the layers of lies I had told myself and releasing the shame and regret I felt for staying so long, the real, beautiful Karen began to emerge. My therapy included writing letters that I would not send—usually to Edgar. I even wrote one to his family, explaining the abuse that I suffered at his hands and begging them not to enable him. I sent it to my printer upstairs and forgot to retrieve it. Jamaal picked up the letter to bring to me. On the way, he glanced at it—and read all the abuse, shame and pain I'd been hiding for years.

Angry and hurt, he yelled, "Mom! I can't believe you were going through this! How could you? Why didn't you tell me? You had me calling this man *Mister*?" Seeing my face, he softened and put his arms around me. "Mom, you are a queen," he gently whispered, as we held each other close. "And if a man can't see that in you, he doesn't deserve you." I wept and wept: my child had to tell me what I should have known all along.

It's been more than three years since the breakup with Edgar— "the breakthrough." At first I was lost, barely able to pick up the pieces of my shattered self-esteem. "When you left Edgar," Jamaal said one day, "you showed me what it means to be strong. You're not alone, Mom." "I know, sweetheart," I said, holding him tight. "And I will never, ever give my power away again." *My* headline will read, "*Dr. Karen Johnson, after many years of searching for love, has found it—in herself.*"

Dr. Karen E. Johnson, a public speaker and women's advocate, is originally from Nassau, Bahamas. With degrees from Howard and Tuskegee Universities, she frequently lectures and has published articles in her field. She has co-authored a medical textbook and is also the author of the forthcoming Bruised on the Inside. *Connect with Dr. Johnson at www. DrKarenEJohnson.com.*

Kris A. Wilkerson

Yes, Mother. Yes.

I don't know what I expected, but it sure wasn't this. Mom's room in the nursing home looked and smelled like a hospital, only worse. There was one bed, though the room had been set up for two, and a dingy imprint remained on the floor where the other bed once stood. An old, yellowed curtain hung limply on a rounded track previously used to separate the beds. My nose wrinkled at the lifeless, musty smell. The walls were the color of a perpetually rainy day, and the flowery accent wallpaper was faded, peeling. My stomach knotted into a ball as I walked in. I smiled for Mom's sake, but I could see from the haunted look in her eyes that she was more heartsick than I. This depressing place was her new home.

The nightmare had started six months before. Until then, Mom had been a youthful sixty-five with an active and vigorous life. She loved to travel, take long walks, work in her garden and participate in her church's many activities. Her favorite adventure was to take her grandkids to Lagoon—a local amusement park— and whoop her way through every ride. Her life sparkled like the clear blue of her aquamarine eyes. But life changed in an instant.

At the family reunion, Mom opted to watch the baby instead of taking even one ride at 3 Kings Amusement Park. I did a mental double-take. The next day, as we walked the airport terminal, I noticed Mom shuffling and panting even though she carried no luggage. "Mom, what's wrong?" She shook her head as the tears welled and she whispered, "Sis, I don't know." I reached to support her, my heart in my throat.

At the hospital, she was misdiagnosed with an autoimmune disease. They pumped her full of steroids before discharging her, but at home her bowel ruptured from the steroids. She had emergency surgery and spent the next three months on life support, her

---

Her life sparkled like the clear blue of her aquamarine eyes. But life changed in an instant.

---

organs on the verge of shutting down. We found ourselves tumbled into the maze of the "long-term healthcare system." Through it all, as decisions were made *for* us; as our questions and concerns were ignored; and as my beautiful, vibrant mother was no longer recognized as a person, I felt a fist of confusion, frustration and anger thudding in the pit of my stomach.

With each interaction, the doctors disconnected further, proclaiming, "Your mom is supposed to be dead, so it won't be long." The fist in my stomach burned like fire as I looked a detached specialist in the eye one day and said with determination, "You don't know my mother; she isn't done yet." He shook his head as if to say, "It's just a matter of time. Can't you see she is as good as dead?" They didn't see Mom. She'd become her diagnosis of someone about to die, and the tasks needed to manage her.

My heart sank as I saw the confusion and frustration in her eyes. I knew this was far more painful for her than the ruptured bowel and surgical wound that landed her in the nursing home. "Why don't they ask me what I want or think? Why do they talk to you, but not me—don't I matter anymore?" Her eyes searched my face for the answer, an answer I now resolved to find. My body and mind were filled with confusion, hurt, anger and the motivation to make things right for my mother.

I listened as we navigated the maze, mentally categorizing the wrongs and beginning to craft solutions. I saw the need to change our collective consciousness of how people treat the elderly and disabled needing long-term care. And it became crystal clear to me that I needed to do something about this tragedy NOW.

The epiphany struck as I sat for the hundredth time in Mom's rain-hued room, my temples throbbing from the scent of decay, my mind screaming with the frustration of the trapped, "Why can't you see her? Why can't you treat her with respect?" Slowly, like the heat of an oil lamp brightening, I realized the change could begin with me. My mom was still alive! She had just as much life, love and purpose to share as any toddler, teenager, or adult. All I had to do was prove it to them and, more importantly, to her.

As a gallery owner, I knew about the impact of environment. I knew that even though my mom's world had been shrunk to a dreary ten-by-twelve space, I could reignite her life by changing her surroundings. I caught my breath, realizing something I

They didn't see Mom. She'd become her diagnosis of someone about to die, and the tasks needed to manage her.

---

already knew—that something so simple and small can have dramatic impact. *Bring life back into her space,* I thought. *Lift her up from the utter despair of this place and then she can fight the system's apathetic diagnosis of "death before you are dead."*

I brought in pieces from my gallery, where my mother had worked and loved the art. Her eyes danced excitedly with a flicker of new life, but I wanted more. I hung up some whimsical gardening pieces. I also brought landscapes, carvings and live green plants. I brought in a bookcase and shelved her books from home, plus her stereo, CDs and DVDs. I cleared the air with oils, candles and fresh flowers. My heart warmed as I saw the life return to Mom's whole being, her eyes and body fully engaged in living again. Her depression lifted immediately. When people are put into long-term care, they're disconnected from society, but art, books and music reconnect them to the joys of everyday life.

Bringing in art was like breathing life into the place. I smiled with satisfaction whenever I saw the nurses and even doctors sneak extra moments in her room to discuss the art. They were visibly affected by the changes. I even caught one doctor whistling a happy tune as he left Mom's room. I, too, felt the changes and began to look forward to my visits.

Mom's health improved so much that she ventured out of her room and began to enjoy the people around her. My heart leapt toward the heavens the first day I walked in her room and saw her standing at an easel, painting her own picture. Betty, one of Mom's nurses, now made extra visits to Mom's room to check the progress of the painting. The joy on Mom's face was a victory like no other I'd ever experienced; she was not just above ground, waiting to die, she was living, laughing and painting. I felt such a surge of warmth and love. Everyone was excited for Mom's daily happiness, and even guardedly hopeful for her recovery.

None of this affected the ultimate outcome, but it completely altered Mom's journey. She felt important again. Just as Mom was beginning to resemble the woman who rode roller coasters, she had another relapse with MRSA infection, which compromises the immune system to the point that organs shut down. Her body slowly wound down. I knew, and she knew, that death was breaths away. We walked her final eight days hand in hand, shoulder to shoulder and heart to heart.

One of my mother's journal entries from that week captured the emotion that filled it. "Every moment, every interaction, is precious and important. Life changes in an instant... sometimes I'm afraid, but more than anything, I am profoundly saddened for those I am leaving behind. My heart aches as I see their grief. I don't know how to ease their pain. I can only tell them, show them, how much I love them. Give them enough love to fill them so even after I'm gone, they feel my love, for it truly is endless."

Because of Mom's tremendous suffering, I'm glad she didn't linger longer; but despite my best attempts to prepare, the grief that visited me gouged deep. I did most of my grieving on the edge of a bluff near my home in Utah. I felt as if that extra-rainy spring was the universe grieving her departure with me. "Why did her suffering have to be so great?" I cried out, as I stood there sobbing one day. Then I heard, coming on the wind, my mother's voice, as clear as the water before me. "Kristine, my sweet, sweet, Sis, this was meant to be. It was my path, as well as yours." My hair

Her depression lifted immediately. When people are put into long-term care, they're disconnected from society, but art, books and music reconnect them to the joys of everyday life.

stood on end and goosebumps rose on my arms. "We agreed to this together," she continued, "and great changes will come from our experience." A sigh escaped my lips as my body relaxed, and a peaceful calm came over me. I knew that this really was the path— her path, as well as mine.

It wasn't long before I saw exactly what she meant by "our path." My experience with her in long-term care had struck a deep chord within me, one that resonated with my overall life mission to create spaces that elevate lives. My new path called me to devote myself to a new vision for long term care living environments—a vision where art, color, lighting, plants and life-enhancing elements are integrated and enjoyed by the elderly and those who care for them. Mine is a vision of quality of life through end of life.

When I create new programs and ways to enrich lives, I feel light surrounding me, embracing me, confirming what I'm doing. And within that light there's always her voice, soft but clear, saying quite simply: "Yes, Sis. This is our path." And I silently respond, "Yes, Mother. Yes."

Kris A. Wilkerson is the Creative Director and founder of Diamond Age World Network (DAWN), a company that is changing long-term care living environments and improving the quality of life for residents, care partners and families. DAWN's team of experts provides long-term care facilities with the solutions they need to make design and physical transformations; they also offer an array of emotional and physical wellness programs. Kris is also the owner of Wilkerson Fine Art and Design, through which she has operated art galleries since 2001 in Huntsville, Eden and Ogden, Utah. The company markets and sells all original art pieces, and creates enriched spaces using color, design and fine art. Connect with Kris at www. WilkersonFineArt.com and www.DAWNera.com.

Beth Rosen, Esq.

Running to the Light

In the rush to the emergency room, traffic lights and street signs flew by in a sickening blur. Every nerve in my body pulsed frenetically as the cold sweat of withdrawal began. My head swam. Just as oblivion was about to consume me, a memory flashed into view from somewhere deep inside. "Remember, Beth," I told myself, "this is who you were before all the trauma, before the endless toxic medications."

A sense of hope and liberation welled up inside me, a promise of release from this drug-induced imprisonment. I saw myself as I once was, beaming at the standing ovation and roaring laughter of the audience for something I had written. Then, just as quickly as it arrived, the vision was gone, replaced by somber reality. We had arrived at the hospital.

Once inside, I was escorted down a cold, dank corridor into a windowless holding room. When I tried to open the door, I found it was locked. A sense of impending doom washed over me as my heart began to race. When the door opened, I gasped at the sight of a nurse wielding a needle the size of Montana. When I protested, "But I'm allergic," she summoned two huge orderlies who strapped me to a chair while kneeling on my frail body. I felt as if my tiny bones would crush beneath their brutish force. I was unable to scream through their suffocating hands as the nurse jabbed the needle into my arm. The sedative worked quickly and the world, once again, became a hazy fog.

But let me back up a bit. This wasn't my normal M.O., and ambulances and I didn't have a long-term relationship. Up to this point, I had been self-possessed and successful. I'd spent years as a spiritual seeker, studying with world-renowned masters of healing and wisdom. My innate sense of justice also led me to become a lawyer. But my beliefs were deeply shaken during a dark period in

---

I couldn't feel anything other than a
sense of being pulled so far inside myself
I wasn't even here anymore.

---

my life. I went for help, spilling out my pain to a therapist. "You have the stuff of genius in you," he told me. "But you can't handle post-traumatic stress disorder alone." This was a slap of reality. I understood that I had suffered real abuse from some of my spiritual teachers, and that I needed healing. I thought the therapist had my best interests at heart when he referred me to a psychiatrist for medication to calm me down.

Strolling home from the therapist's office, I mulled it over. *Should I try Western medicine?* Trained in Eastern spiritual practices, I'd come to view the mind and body as an integrated whole. I usually shunned even the mildest painkillers. But out of desperation, I decided to trust—to try medication.

I approached the psychiatrist's office with misgivings. After a short consultation, she reached for her prescription pad. *So soon?* I thought. *She didn't even ask about my medical history, or much of anything.* I shook as I read the diagnosis: "Psychosis." I understood what this meant: a mental disorder characterized by delusions, personality disintegration and irrational thoughts. *Crazy,* I thought. *She thinks I'm crazy.*

The word cut through me like a knife and sent shivers down my spine. Somehow, the queasiness in my gut and her shocking diagnosis rekindled the pain of my earlier emotional and physical abuse. As I was flooded with haunting memories, I regressed into a state of disempowerment. Every ounce of me screamed, "Get out now!" But I was speechless as my knees buckled beneath me. Unable to think clearly, I filled the prescription—the final relinquishment of my own free will.

Month after medicated month passed. Soon I was hopelessly addicted, but still suffering from my original symptoms. On doctor's orders, I continued to take medicine that paralyzed my face into a permanent frown and shut down my capacity to think. I could no longer feel my arms or legs.

I, who had once run marathons and danced with joy, was now reduced to a life of trembling, barely able to move or put a coherent sentence together. I couldn't feel anything other than a sense of being pulled so far inside myself I wasn't even here anymore.

Soon, that's the way the world began to treat me. I no longer laughed, no longer spoke. I withdrew into a world of suffering.

It was like God entering my broken heart.

As my isolation increased, so did my depression. By the time my medications had been tripled, I was itching for release. When my psychiatrist refused to wean me off the drugs, I decided to do it myself, cold turkey. That's how I landed in the emergency room.

After my hospital visit, my psychiatrist prescribed ever-stronger drugs—cocktails of antipsychotics and antidepressants that plunged me into a zombie-like stupor. I gained forty-five pounds.

My days were spent curled up in a ball, sleeping eighteen hours at a time, trying to escape the monotonous drone in my head. My nights were even worse, wracked by hallucinations and nightmares. Incoherent, numb and terrified, I rarely ventured outside the house. Even my husband's love couldn't reach through the stupor.

Lying in bed one day, I thought, *I'm done. I give up. Death would be better than this, and I'm ready to just end it all.* I wanted to stop being a burden to my husband. Ready for anything, I started to let go, surrendering into the abyss of sorrow. Suddenly, I saw a flash of white light and felt an eerie stillness come over me. It calmed and comforted me, if only for a brief moment. It was like God entering my broken heart.

Then, I felt an electrifying spark, as my spirit came alive for the first time in years. It was a call to arms. I was instantly able to grab onto some piece of me that hadn't died. I clung tightly to this small bright light as I clawed my way back from the doors of death.

The next day was prescription day, the one day I left the house. I dragged myself listlessly to the drugstore. The pharmacist looked at my prescription, then at me, then back at my prescription. "Ms. Rosen," she said haltingly, "This isn't right. This dosage is dangerously high." Her concern reached through my mental miasma. *Someone had recognized me. Someone cared.* The fog had dissipated just a tiny bit more.

It was time to get off the medication. I knew this now. Because of my frightening cold turkey experience, I realized I had to do it in stages. It was everything I could do to lace up my jogging shoes for the first time in years with the sedatives still coursing through my body. I ran slowly at first, gradually picking up speed. My husband stood by me, coaxing me on. "You can do it. You're an

---

As I reconnected to love, I reconnected to myself.

---

athlete!" The weight began to slough off as I broke free of the drug-induced stupor. With each inhale, I imagined I was breathing in the bright shiny Beth I used to be; with each exhale, I expelled the dense blanket of fog that consumed my spirit. My jogs became six-mile runs, the wind at my back and a taste of freedom in my heart.

My next visit to the psychiatrist would be my last. I was going to take control of my life: no more medicine. I would step back into my power and live in the light, even if I had to turn it on myself. I attended enlightenment camps, where I met wonderful and supportive people. They, along with my husband, became my touchstones during those dicey periods of withdrawal.

As I reconnected to love, I reconnected to myself. I gained further clarity and peace when I switched to a vegan diet after recognizing my food allergy to eggs and dairy products. I now began to enjoy yoga, dancing and running. As my face unfroze from its medically-induced paralysis, I began to smile from deep within and my playful spirit re-emerged. I brought myself up to speed in my field of legal expertise, started a legal consulting business and became an author, a screenwriter and a film producer, my life's passion.

As I reflect on my journey back to myself, a sense of sadness washes over me. But I treasure my newfound wisdom and appreciation for the things that really matter in life—friends, family, nature and the wherewithal to truly come from the spirit within and live one's dream no matter what. You can't change the past, but you can get past it.

Every so often, when I am running by the water, heart pumping, feet pounding, I hear the distant siren of an ambulance and remember that long-ago ride to the emergency room. Words cannot express the joy I feel as I drink in the salty air and recall how I broke free, how I earned freedom, and how I work every day to keep it. This is the wellspring of my gratitude, as I excitedly propel myself forward into uncharted waters.

Beth Rosen, Esq., is an attorney, a healer, a professor of yoga, an author, an illustrator, a comedy writer, a screenwriter, a songwriter, a film producer and an actress. She graduated from Columbia Law School and the Wharton School of Business, and owns her own production company, Signature Beth Productions, LLC.

Beth spent ten years studying with various masters in such disciplines as spirituality, healing, yoga, martial arts and business. Her creative endeavors reflect an integration of the life-enhancing philosophies of the East with the fast-paced modalities of the West, striving to get to the heart of the matter and touch the soul in profound ways. Her current project is a book on enlightenment, It Does Matter and So Do You: You Can Change the World if You Get Back In It. *Connect with Beth at www.BethRosen. com and www.EnlightenmentIsHere.com.*

Christie Mawer

Birth of the Bad Kitty

I sat hunched in my sister's basement, blue light from the computer screen zapping my bloodshot eyes. I'd been scanning my queue of online dating sites for hours. The whole night—and most of the day—had passed as I checked my inboxes, flirted, chatted, winked, poked, planned clandestine meetings and flat-out obsessed over my need to find love again. I needed a little something, preferably over six feet tall, to drag my badly charred self-esteem up from out of the ashes.

Being cheated on had made me feel so rejected, so unlovable, I looked in the mirror and saw a big nothing. And, it's depressing as hell to live in your sister's basement. Cold and dark, my bedroom was my nine-year-old nephew's room, empty for the summer, decorated in bright boy colors, with model cars and Transformers on the shelves and a little skinny kid's bed. If I stretched out all the way, my ankles hung over its edge. One tiny window let in a faint light.

I felt so lost—I didn't know how to occupy myself without love, or without sex. These were the only things that made me feel like a whole woman. Even while I looked for love online, I obsessed about Joe.

I'd met Joe—a photographer in his mid-forties who had never married or had children—five years before. We had had some intense experiences together. I thought we had grown quite emotionally, spiritually and physically close. He was my man, and I was his woman. We were committed—or so I thought.

On his birthday, I sat at home for hours waiting for him to get back from a photo shoot. By eleven, I was in full stew mode. I could feel cartoon steam coming out of my ears and knots of worry in my gut. *It's his birthday, for God's sake.* I nodded off on the couch as I waited with scenarios of what was wrong swirling in my head.

I needed a little something, preferably over six feet tall, to drag my badly charred self-esteem up from out of the ashes.

When I woke, around two in the morning, still no Joe. My concern turned to anger, and I started vibrating. "That's it," I shouted to the empty room. "Fifteen more minutes and I'm barring the door!"

Twelve minutes later, Joe walked in. I was grateful to see him alive but still fuming at the same time. He avoided my eyes and rattled off his "sorries," a list of excuses for why he'd been late and what snafus had occurred at the shoot with Monique. Everything in my body started to scream that something was very, very wrong. Some part of him, some big special part, wasn't with me anymore. When we climbed into bed, I pushed the feeling away. I didn't want to look at it—I needed him too badly to make me feel beautiful and show me I was whole.

During the months that followed, an invisible wall followed us around. Eventually we broke up. Neither of us wanted to leave our small house, so we continued to live together and sleep in the same bed. Though I didn't admit it, I didn't know if I could live without Joe. I hoped that if we kept living together, he would change his mind. I had no outer validation for this idea. It was simply easier to ignore reality.

And then one night, as we took a walk by the river, I had to ask. "Are you fooling around with Monique?" "Yes," he answered. My glass house shattered with a loud crash. I started shaking. Despite my fear, I had to ask the next question. "How long has this been happening?" I sounded remarkably calm. "About eight months." *Eight months? That's a long-term relationship! I've been sleeping with another woman's man!*

I felt like a Mack truck hit me in my gut, and all I could see was red taillights as it drove away, carrying my life with it. My pent-up frustration erupted. With all the strength of my full-figured six feet, I pushed him. His watch flew off. I picked it up and hurled it toward the river. If I had been able to pick *him* up, I would have tossed his ass right after it.

Immediately, I moved out and went to stay in my sister's basement, where I languished in my blue screen fantasy world. I was so angry with myself—I had failed, even though I'd tried to do everything right.

One day, I said to myself, "This is stupid. I am not going to freeze in this basement for one more minute while he's all warm and cushy in that house." I drove over to demand he leave. I was vibrating with such anger and resentment, I don't know how I managed to drive. I could almost hear the movie revenge music playing in the background. Justice will be served!

I was concerned I might be judged,
but more excited about what the
party could mean for all of us.

When I saw him, I suddenly realized: *I don't even want the house. I don't want the memories, I don't want the drama. I want to be validated. I want the warmth of being loved.* The chill of the basement had nothing to do with temperature—it was the chill of being rejected and unloved. In that moment, I began bawling uncontrollably, falling to the floor and curling up into the fetal position. I screamed for all the times I'd ever settled, all the times I'd sacrificed and performed. I screamed for all the energy and authenticity it had cost me. As I let go, I felt a sense of rebirth. Though I was embarrassed to be doing it on the floor in front of

Joe, I had already gone too far to stop. This breaking through was about me. Knowing what I was experiencing, Joe was gentle and kind and nurtured me through it.

Coming to his home didn't have much to do with him. It had everything to do with me finding myself. As I drove away from Joe's house, I realized it didn't matter who I was with, Joe or one of those guys I'd met online. The common ingredient in every equation had always been me, needing a man to validate my beauty. I realized

---

Watching each of my girlfriends give herself permission to embrace and express her whole self, too, I was clear it wasn't the pole-dancing I was so excited about. It was the opportunity it gave each of us.

---

that I had to *own* the warmth I had felt in what was once our home. It had to come with me wherever I went. My whole being began to clear again. When I returned to my sister's basement, I returned more empowered and whole than I'd ever felt.

Around this time, I heard a documentary about pole-dancing parties, and my ears perked right up. The women they interviewed sounded joyful and empowered. People associate pole dancing with pleasing men, but here were women having a great time being girly, being theatrical, being silly, getting out of their comfort zones and allowing themselves self-love and sensuality without judging themselves or each other. There were no men anywhere! Hallelujah!

With my sister's blessing, I ordered my pole and instructional DVD and planned a party of my own, inviting all my friends. I was concerned I might be judged, but more excited about what the party could mean for all of us.

Much to my distress, my stuff was delayed and I had to learn all the moves in two days! With trepidation, and a lot of excitement about this new opportunity for self-discovery, I went to work. After one full day of training, I thought I'd better wear black and blue to the party to match all my bruises. I don't exercise. I won't run unless I'm in physical danger, and even then I'll think twice. I was in pain! My body ached, yet my heart, mind and spirit were soaring, light as a butterfly. Unbelievable: here I was doing for me what I had done for so many men—and feeling more complete than I'd ever felt. I loved it! Most surprisingly, despite my tendency to be distracted by the "next fun, shiny thing," I stuck with it.

Pole dancing incorporates all the things I love to do best: performing, teaching, being out in the limelight and watching people transform. At my first pole-dancing party, there with my best girls, all of us sparkling with energy and having fun, I discovered I had a gift. I felt so beautiful expressing my whole self. Watching each of my girlfriends give herself permission to embrace and express her whole self, too, I was clear it wasn't the pole-dancing I was so excited about. It was the opportunity it gave each of us.

Who would have thought a pole would be about personal discovery, instead of a phallic symbol? Who would have thought the simple act of dancing would have been about me—and other women—being comfortable in our own skin, without the presence of a man? Who would have thought it would allow me to laugh again, and share healthy intimacy with women and girlfriends? I no longer had to stay online twenty-four hours a day peering through bloodshot eyes searching for intimacy. Who would have thought a "stripper's" pole would mean total liberation and self discovery? Sensuality could be just for fun. It could be just for me.

Now, when I look in the mirror, I purr in satisfaction like a cat stretched in the sun. I have found a purpose beyond pleasing a man, in teaching women self-development through sensual dance. There is nothing like kicking up our high heels in joyful play and loving ourselves just as we are!

Christie Mawer's passion is to help other women discover their own authentic expression. She believes that sensuality—living through the senses—is at the core of authenticity. Drawing on her background in public speaking, theater and dance, Christie developed a unique business called The Bad Kitty, which creates safe, fun space for women to become empowered in rediscovering and embracing themselves and the full expression of their authentic sensuality through a combination of self-development work and sensual dance. Christie wants every woman to live by the motto: BE BEAUTIFUL, BE YOU! Connect with Christie at www.TheBadKitty.com.

Andrea Ross

Adrenalin Peaked

S ummer, 2008: Everything depends, in this moment, on my
being able to successfully parallel-park—blindfolded—on a
busy street in downtown Calgary.

I am in the middle of the infamous City Chase, a blast of a
race that has us sprinting Calgary's city streets and rushing to
local transit in an effort to rack up points via a series of physical,
intellectual and fear-based challenges. We have six hours to
complete the race. Most people are happy just to participate, but
I'm in it to win.

This year, CBC has chosen my two-person team to film for
reality TV. We wear mics and battery packs, and a camera crew
drives beside us, trying to keep up as we zip around town like
mad.

We roller-derby. We run to Fort Calgary, where we have to
dress up and answer historical trivia questions. We dash to 17th
Avenue, where we eat hot dogs with disgusting toppings (escargot,
sauerkraut, Captain Crunch). I take off my shoes and jump into a
pool of pasta to find a key and open a box with a menu in it, then
memorize menu items. We carry guns while crawling through
mud, rolling tires and climbing ropes, all while soldiers yell at us at
the tops of their lungs. I feel the familiar rush of adrenalin pushing
me to go faster, faster, faster.

The final challenge is WWF wrestling, which just happened to be my favorite as a kid. The professional wrestlers are stunned when I flip them with my leg wrestle and fly through the air with a drop-elbow. We're almost there! I can hear someone shouting, "You've got it, this race is yours!" We cross the finish line, fists pumping, screaming with excitement: "We won! We won!"

We've torn it up in just over two hours and seventeen minutes! Adrenalin pumps joy all over my body. And as the camera crew re-films us doing parts of the race, I am already thinking about my *next* race, Full Moon in June, a thirty-six-hour hiking, biking,

---

I had no idea that, on that triumphant day,
I was—quite literally—in a coma. Adventure
girl, it turns out, was living on pure adrenalin.

---

kayaking, rappelling and orienteering extravaganza. Plus, I'm going to Chicago in a few days. There's so much to do before I go. I need more time to train—I need to pack—

I had no idea that, on that triumphant day, I was—quite literally—in a coma. Adventure girl, it turns out, was living on pure adrenalin. Months after City Chase and Full Moon in June, I went to a naturopath for help with my allergies. Through a series of odd tests, he discovered an unrelated ailment; I had adrenal fatigue. My exhausted adrenal glands were unable to produce adequate quantities of hormones, primarily cortisol. I had excessively low DHEA, estrogen and progesterone. "I don't even understand how you get out of bed in the morning," the doctor said. "With hormone levels like yours, you should be in a coma." Whoa. No wonder I craved adrenalin.

"Unless you increase your hormone levels," he went on, "you won't be able to have children." "What?" I cried. My emotions bubbled over, and tears spilled down my cheeks. At thirty-two, I didn't know if I wanted to have kids, but I sure as hell wanted to have the opportunity. I thought I was winning everything—now I felt like the ultimate failure. "You have to slow down, right now," the doctor said. But I was never still, not for an instant. Something had to change, but how? I ran a thousand miles per hour *all* the time.

I don't know where my drive came from, but only the best would do for me since at least age three, when I concentrated obsessively on racking up points in preschool for spelling words correctly. In first grade, I competed to get the best grades on tests. It was the same all the way through school, but no one else was competing with me—I was just competing with myself.

Then I became an engineer, and started shooting up the corporate ladder. I didn't even enjoy engineering, but others had told me, "You should do this. You need to get a good-paying job." I desired approval from everyone; it validated my existence and allowed me to feel better about myself. Having credentials and a difficult degree earned me immediate respect; having money

---

Being who and doing what others thought I "should" meant I would be liked. Excelling at things meant I would be a success...or would it?

---

would buy me stuff that would impress others; who cared if I hated my job? I could be happy on evenings and weekends. At that point I didn't realize the only one I needed approval from was myself. Being who and doing what others thought I "should" meant I would be liked. Excelling at things meant I would be a success... or would it?

I scheduled every spare second of my life *doing*. I worked out every day, took a multitude of diverse classes and worked on side projects—it wasn't enough just to be an engineer, I also had to have my own companies. I had to be better, be successful, achieve. Every weekend was planned with adventure races, training, travel, kayaking lessons—if you wanted to go for coffee with me, you had to book me three months in advance.

There was no time left to be spontaneous, no time to relax, no time to get bored; every moment of every day was jam-packed.

Success was an impossible feat when my bar moved higher with every accomplishment. My high expectations were destroying me.

Above all, I have always been an adventure-girl. I'm one of those people who, if I died tomorrow, would have lived my life with no regrets; you should see my Bucket List. I've been in crazy races and on wild adventures all over the world, running with the bulls in Pamplona and doing a pseudo-Houdini with Richard Branson, who wrapped me up in chains, locked me up and threw snakes on me while dangling the keys to my captivity over my head. I have even eaten fire!

So stop racing? Stop working out? Stop working? What else was there? I was mortified. I had rarely even taken a sick day. Even if I were on my deathbed, I'd go in to work. I didn't think about the fact that my co-workers would hate me for making them sick. I just thought, "I'm so great, I'm so strong, I can be sick and still work!" I didn't know how to take a break. And I sure didn't know how to face anyone with this information; it was too personal. It made me look weak.

The day I told my boss, I was sick to my stomach. I felt so embarrassed about being sick. I cried all weekend, afraid to admit I needed time off work. What would I do? I walked to his office a couple times, but turned back in fear. It was bonus time, and I only got the courage up to tell him when he came into my office to give me my bonus. Until that moment, I kept putting it off. "It's not serious," I said. If I downplayed it, I might not seem like such a failure. The guys at work were angry; they thought I was taking a fake sick leave and just couldn't hack it, that I was taking my bonus and a little vacation. No one cared to understand or even ask what was wrong—but I didn't want to explain myself, either. I imagined myself, just "one of the guys," walking into that money-oriented, male-dominated office and talking about my hormone imbalances and my inability to have children. It just wasn't going to happen.

I thought I was wrong to take care of myself—and so did my company. They let me go. Mingled with my feelings of shock, anger, fear and confusion, though, was a sense of relief. For the first time in my life, someone had given me permission to take a break, to take time for me.

I knew my sick leave would be the end of my career. And sure enough, it was. But really, it was the best thing that ever happened to me. Now that I had time to be with myself, I started to discover the belief system that had been driving me forward at such high

---

I knew my sick leave would be the end of my career. And sure enough, it was. But really, it was the best thing that ever happened to me.

---

speeds; *I'm not good enough.* Over the next year I pulled back the throttle; I learned to slow down and surrender. I started asking myself questions that had been too long ignored: What am I up to, anyway? What am I trying to prove? What is success? What if I "win" and get to the top of that corporate ladder but find myself alone without love and family? What *is* really important in life?

Summer, 2010: City Chase is total mayhem. All around me, people are cheering, shouting and tearing about in the sunshine. I however, am walking! Who'd have thought I'd be here just to enjoy the day? I could win this race; I organized it in 2009, I know all its ins and outs. But my friend and I just stroll the city at an easy pace, enjoying each challenge and soaking up the gorgeous day. No pressure to win feels really good.

I find myself, several times, starting to run. And each time I slow myself down and enjoy the moment. At this pace, the world seems more vivid, full of color. This is anything but failure. Even without the race, the win, the rush of adrenalin, I'm good enough, and I always have been.

Andrea Ross is an adventurpreneur: an adventurer, explorer and entrepreneur who thrives on adrenalin, love, fun and discovery. An MBA and professional engineer, Andrea abandoned her "being better than the Joneses" lifestyle to pursue her passions for inspiring others through leadership, adventure and excitement (www.AdrenalinPeak.com). Andrea has traveled to forty-nine countries (so far), organized and participated in adventure races around the world, pitched an idea on the Dragon's Den, been hit by a train and been kissed by Steven Tyler of Aerosmith. Richard Branson named her Canada's "Most Fearless Woman." Read her blog at www.Adventurpreneur.wordpress.com for more great stories!

Carole Miville

Living to Laugh, Laughing to Live

"W hy doesn't God just come pick me up?" my mother asked. We were in her apartment, her fifth in two years. Because of a misdiagnosis, she'd been caught in a medical/bureaucratic nightmare, and I'd moved her from place to place to place. This apartment was nice—small and manageable, with a lovely balcony and a kitchen bathed in sunshine every morning. But Mom was eighty-five and angry and couldn't enjoy anything.

"Would it be so hard for God to take me?" she asked. "No, it wouldn't," I said, "but He doesn't want you at this moment. Heaven is a place for happy people, and you're too angry. Nobody wants you around now, not even God. You'd just be a party pooper up there." I could see her resisting the laughter, fighting it off, but she couldn't help herself. She laughed. Aha! There was the laugh I remembered—the laugh I had to work desperately to earn these days from the very woman who had given me her sense of humor, the very woman who had earned the nickname Mrs. Smiles. Just six years ago, Mrs. Smiles loved to read, go to the movies and even go downtown by herself to eat at bars. She was full of life and laughter, but that was *then*.

One day, talking with my mom on the phone, I noticed she was speaking more slowly than usual and seemed confused. I jumped in my car and drove to her house. When I said, "Mom, I'm taking you to the hospital," she seemed afraid to go, but I took her anyway.

After a lot of tests, the doctors came into her room, pulled back the curtain and said the words that would change our lives: "Your mother has Alzheimer's disease." When I asked the doctor how he came to that conclusion, he said it was because she was having trouble with her memory.

"Of course she's having trouble with her memory," I said. "She's eighty-five years old. Most people her age need ten minutes to remember the name of their favorite actor—even if it's Brad Pitt!" I knew it was impossible that my mother had Alzheimer's, but I ignored my intuition and listened to the doctors. I felt I had no choice.

They admitted her to the hospital so they could run more tests. All day long, different doctors and nurses came and asked her the

> I knew it was impossible that my mother had Alzheimer's, but I ignored my intuition and listened to the doctors. I felt I had no choice.

same questions repeatedly to test her memory: What's your name? What's your address? How many kids do you have? "They ask the same questions over and over. I'm tired of it," Mom said. "Next time," I told her, "ask them if *they're* the ones with Alzheimer's."

Still, they determined she had Alzheimer's, so they gave her another test to see if she could live by herself. As she took her test, I sat in the waiting room, wondering what in the world was going to happen to my mother. She didn't have Alzheimer's—I just knew it! But what were we going to do?

Full of frustration, mulling over what the tests might show, I wondered to myself why waiting rooms were so boring. "You all should paint this room pink and hang a huge piñata," I mused to the nurse when she walked in. "Before patients go back to see their doctors, they can take a swing at the piñata." She didn't see the humor in my suggestion, and I went back to waiting, wishing there was a piñata in front of me to smack so I could relieve some of the stress of not knowing.

After a couple of hours, Mom came shuffling into the room, accompanied by a nurse. She looked pretty downcast. "I failed," she said. "How could you possibly fail?" I said. "It was a cooking test," she said, "and they think I've forgotten how to cook." "Forgotten?" I said to the nurse who accompanied her. "She never knew. She would have failed that test at the age of twenty-five, let alone eighty-five."

They ignored my protests and moved her into a nursing-home type residence with a bunch of other people who actually did have Alzheimer's. "Why am I here?" she asked. "I don't have Alzheimer's." Because of her work as a nurse, she knew all about the diseases that visit the aged, and she knew, as I did, that she did not have Alzheimer's. I pled her case with the doctors, but the only thing I could do was move her to an area where visiting nurses came by every day. One day, after Mom had been in the nursing home for fourteen weeks, the words that we had been silently praying for fell from one nurse's lips. "Your mom doesn't have Alzheimer's. She's depressed, but she doesn't have Alzheimer's."

Infuriated, yet relieved, I said we should move her back to her original home to alleviate the depression. The nurse agreed, but said we needed to get medical verification from a psychiatrist. The psychiatrist confirmed our nurse's diagnosis.

When my mother heard this, she completely lost her temper. She looked the doctor right in the eye and yelled, loud enough so that everyone in the waiting room could hear her, "Do you realize how this mistake has ruined my life? This is the last time I will see a doctor in my life. I don't trust any one of you anymore!" She stormed out of the office. We both cried all the way home.

We moved her back into her original home. I spent so much time taking care of her. I helped her with shopping, cooking, laundry and cleaning the house. I was becoming her mom. We both cried the first time I had to give her a bath. She didn't like being dependent, so she always refused my help. I would ask her if I could do something, and she always said, "No." I told a friend that growing old is like being a child again, and my mom was in her "no" phase!

Ironically, I was speaking at conferences, telling people how to bring humor into their own lives while I was trying to figure out how bring humor into this nightmare I was living with my mother. I was exhausted and beginning to wonder if I had caught some of her depression. But the minute I got on stage, the act of teaching others how to laugh in difficult circumstances forced me to do the same. And that's what made my humor genuine and effective. I was practicing what I preached, even as I preached it.

I gave my mother permission to vent her emotions, but it was impossible for me to listen to it every day. So when she phoned me to rant, I'd set the phone down away from my ear and let her rant. Sometimes, I'd do some other activity while she ranted, and when the phone became silent, I knew she was done. That's when I picked the phone back up and talked with her.

One day, she called and said, "I've had it. I'm going to jump off of my balcony." I wanted to lift her up, so I tried a joke. "Don't be stupid, Mom. Your apartment is on the second floor! It's not nearly

---

I would ask her if I could do something,
and she always said, "No." I told a friend
that growing old is like being a child again,
and my mom was in her "no" phase!

---

high enough to kill yourself. You'll just break a leg and have to go back to the hospital." She didn't laugh at that one, but inside, I did. Sometimes, in order to be able to laugh about something, you first have to be able to cry. With my mother, I so often had to let go of all the sadness and anger in order to make space for joy. I used humor to ease the sadness. It helped me survive!

As I spoke at my conferences, I became increasingly aware that my most important audience member was myself. Life was so hard that I needed to remind myself how to laugh. I told the audience (and myself) about how important it is to seek out humor. I told them (and myself) to look for good comedy shows on TV, read the comics in the papers, avoid negative news and seek funny people to be around, since our thoughts lead to our emotions.

My humor was working, for both me *and* my mother. At least, we were both laughing. Not all of the time. Some days I was just

---

Sometimes, in order to be able to laugh about something, you first have to be able to cry. With my mother, I so often had to let go of all the sadness and anger in order to make space for joy. I used humor to ease the sadness. It helped me survive!

---

too overwhelmed, and some days, so was she. "No jokes," she'd say on those days. "I'm not laughing today. I'm in a mood." Humor is about balance. It doesn't overcome the negative in our lives; it can't. It just counteracts it, keeping our inner scales even.

In February 2010, my mother succumbed to her illness–the one that was misdiagnosed. It was the misdiagnosis that led her into the depression that she really never overcame. Fortunately for both of us, she had taught me from an early age to maintain my balance with humor; and to her credit, she taught me well enough that her last years, while sometimes painfully depressing and exhausting, were still tinged with laughter.

And it's the laughter that I'll remember, as I imagine her finally finding peace and laughing her way through the pearly gates, especially when she hears how I answered the funeral director when he asked whether I wanted a plastic or wooden urn: "It has to be the wooden urn—she hated Tupperware!"

Carole Miville is a singer, entertainer and humorist. She graduated from the National School of Humor in Montreal in 1991. Her interest in personal development has always been central to her personal and professional concerns. In 2000, Carole created a conference titled "Laugh and Grow," which challenges assumptions about what it means to be "productive" in the workplace and encourages people to use humor in the office. Over the years, she has presented this seminar to several hundred organizations.

In 2007, Carole discovered the concept of "edutainment," a learning process that encompasses the mental, physical, emotional and spiritual dimensions of all human beings. And in 2008, after an unforgettable training with Peak Potentials, one of the largest success training companies in North America, she launched her own international practice in India with the Indian Noni Family. Carole was invited back to India in 2009 for the World Wellness Women's Congress, where she was in the same program with Bob Proctor. She is the author of two books, including Laugh and Grow!, *which shares the tools she has used to create happiness in her life and the lives of others. Connect with Carole at www.Laugh-And-Grow. com.*

Cindy Yip

A Single Step

I am the oldest of four children raised in a typical Chinese home in Vancouver, Canada. Ours was a joyous and stable household, and I knew we were expected to conform to our community's expectations: go to university, graduate, establish a career, marry, buy a house and have two kids. All in all, a pretty conventional life plan, one that spans many cultures — but a cookie-cutter life nonetheless.

My first boyfriend was the first indication that conforming to cookie-cutter expectations was not in my future. I was fourteen, and he was the wrong boyfriend, or so my parents thought. He was in his second year at university, so he was significantly older than me. We also had the same last name, which meant that, at some point in the deep past, our ancestors were related. My parents were livid. We fought endlessly, and at one point they said, "If you don't like it, you can get out."

Those three months my boyfriend and I dated were dark times. I lived in the gloomiest of shadows and felt the bleakest of despair. I was in chaos—so lost, so weak, and so alone. No one loved me, and everyone was against me. My boyfriend did not help matters. "Your parents don't love you," he told me one night in his car. "Your siblings don't love you. Nobody in the whole world loves you except me." Too weak to hold up my head, I laid it on his chest. Completely lacking in any self-confidence, I thought: *He's right.*

Every day, I felt an unbearable hollowness. Life is supposed to be fun, and it had been, until I met him. *Why are you wallowing in misery?* I asked myself. *You only feel worse after seeing him. Could Mom and Dad be right? Are his intentions less than good? This relationship has no potential, and aren't you tired of playing the puppet?* I kept listening for my own voice, within, for the right response. But I had no voice. Out of self-preservation, I escaped my prisoner's cell of despair and finally left him, but it wasn't because of any sound within. It was only the noise without.

> *All in all, a pretty conventional life plan, one that spans many cultures—but a cookie-cutter life nonetheless.*

Just because I was free did not mean I was confident. My boyfriend had intentionally trampled my self-confidence, and as I slowly rebuilt myself, I only felt ready to play it safe. Conformity is a disastrous standard to apply in pursuing a relationship.

I met Steven at a Chinese cultural society in Vancouver. It was one of many such clubs established by China's earliest immigrants to the West as places to meet and preserve our Chinese culture and heritage. At the time, our club was hosting a Kung Fu master from China who had come to teach martial arts. "Why don't you guys go there for lessons," my dad said to my siblings and me. "It will be a great way to exercise and hang out with other kids." We agreed.

Steven joined the martial arts classes soon after I did. I was smitten from the first moment he walked into class. He was so cute, and he had a confidence that made it seem like he floated into the room. I'd never seen anyone stand so straight. He became enamored of me, and subtly pursued me.

A few weeks later, as we were walking out of class, he said, "Cindy, can I ask you something?" "Sure," I said, my mouth dry with nervousness. He led me over to a corner where we were—sort of—alone. "Do you want to go out to dinner or something?" he asked, so casual, so suave, as if he weren't nervous at all. It took everything I had not to leap through the ceiling with joy. "That'd be great," I said.

We went to dinner and spoke excitedly about our lives and passions. Everything felt fresh and electrifying. Over the ensuing months, he sent me flowers and poems regularly. We went to different high schools, and after school, he drove over to mine to pick me up and take me home. I had a job at the mall, and he knew my schedule, so he would show up when I was off and we would go out to a movie or dinner. Most importantly, my parents liked him, and his parents loved me. Steven and I were everything our parents thought our future spouses should be. I didn't even bother to listen for the voice telling me what I thought.

I enrolled in university, and majored in English and history. I immersed myself in poetry, prose, and past events. I reveled in Chaucer, Brontë, Austen, Shakespeare and so many others. In one class, we read Thoreau's *Walden,* where I came across the line, "The mass of men lead lives of quiet desperation."

I was strangely drawn to this text, and the possibility that people are miserable because they chain themselves to lives filled with miserable jobs and unrewarding obligations in order to pursue material comforts. I began to wonder if I was one of those people he said were doing what they were doing because society said they should—one of those people who never questioned the order and arrangement of things, or looked deep within to find what really mattered to them. Could I be one of them?

I was so enthralled with all of these ideas that I shared them with Steven, but he just shrugged. All he ever wanted to talk about was high school and cars. I wondered which friends I could call and talk to. *None,* I realized with a pang. *You phased them all out long ago so that you could have more room for Steven.* Realizing, now, how alone I was, I can honestly say I was mortified the night it unraveled with Steven. I guess I should have seen it coming. He always had a short temper, and when he snapped, it was over inconsequential things—the jeans I wore were too faded, the chocolate cake I baked wasn't sweet enough, the movies I loved were too stupid. And yet, we plodded on because we did not know how to do otherwise. It was just assumed that we were going to marry, and neither of us questioned it... until that night.

I was in the living room, watching TV. He came in and told me to change the channel. Thinking nothing of it, I decided to finish the funny commercial I was watching and said, "In a minute." Before I knew what was happening, he had grabbed the remote and thrown it across the room. "When I want you to change the goddamned channel, you change the goddamned channel."

I ran to the kitchen, not because I was afraid he would physically abuse me, but because I was furious and hurt. My fury was red hot and burning, and my pain felt like a mortal wound. It was like a tornado had just ripped right through me. Then it all disappeared, and there was silence. In that silence, it became crystal clear what I had to do. It was over. I told him to get out. He stood there for a minute, and I shouted, "Get out of the house right now." He paused before he turned, but finally left without even saying he was sorry.

The relationship was over, but you don't end a ten-year relationship overnight. I wanted to soften the blow. "Steven," I said, a few nights later. "I think we need to take a break." We sat on his parents' back porch on a warm September evening. "I am not

---

It was only one step, but it put me on the right path. And on that path, I could hear something faint in the distance. I could hear my own voice. I could hear my future.

---

sure our relationship is working anymore, so I would like to take a break for three months. After some time apart, we can reevaluate where we are going." He was not happy about it, but he did not think I was actually breaking up with him, so he agreed to it.

It was only one step, but it put me on the right path. And on that path, I could hear something faint in the distance. I could hear my own voice. I could hear my future. My life changed dramatically, immediately, forever. I now see that I was not only breaking up with Steven, I was also breaking up with my life of utter conformity. I knew that I was one of those people Thoreau was talking about. To pursue material comforts and maintain the peace, I had chained

---

My life, which had seemed so secure, so set, so dull, now sparkled like a diamond— my very own precious gem of a life.

---

myself to a life with a miserable job and unrewarding obligations to Steven and my family. I had never questioned the order or arrangement of things. I had never looked deep within to figure out what really mattered to me.

I had lived the life others expected me to live for so long that taking one step away from that path inspired me to take one more, and then another, and then another, until soon I found myself with a brand new life.

The process of self-discovery was really scary at first; being alone for the first time in my adult life, pursuing *my* interests, *my* passions. My cure was to jam-pack my schedule. I signed up for a Latin dance class at the local community center, and I loved it. I immersed myself in dancing and even joined a dance team. I rebuilt old friendships, and one of them was with a girl who worked as a stewardess. I traveled all over the world with her. I got active in the community, and volunteered for numerous leadership roles. My life, which had seemed so secure, so set, so dull, now sparkled like a diamond—my very own precious gem of a life.

I did eventually meet with Steven to break it off completely, but by then I was so immersed in my new life that the breakup was anti-climactic. And to my surprise, I had my family's support. I explained my breakup to my parents, and Dad said, "I love you, dear, and I will support you in whatever you choose." What a relief! What an unexpected blessing! I could live my life on my terms AND have the support of my family? I saw in that moment that society's rules and ideas — and my parents — weren't all that bad. It was my blind allegiance to all of it that made it impossible for me to find myself, until I realized that "normal" and "cookie-cutter" just wouldn't do for me. They didn't feel good anymore.

I am blessed to have found me — and my sparkling future— because I paid attention to what didn't feel good and walked away from it, one step at a time. Everything I say I know is true, because I heard my voice, my inner voice, telling me so.

Cindy Yip is a successful real estate investor and a Master NLP practitioner. She is also a passionate salsa and ballroom dancer who danced competitively. Cindy has published Cindy's Sparkling Steps, *a monthly newsletter she uses to share her experiences, thoughts, information and ideas with thousands of readers. Connect with Cindy at www.SparklingCindy.com.*

Katherine Lia

The Blessing of Heartbreak

It's a mild August morning in 2001, an hour or so before dawn. To Addie and Charlie, the world must seem very quiet. We are standing on the lawn, waiting for our house to blow up. Only I know this is about to happen; the kids are simply tired and disoriented, leaning against me and mumbling as they drift in and out of sleep.

"What's happening, Mommy?"

I try to maintain an outward calm. "Don't worry, sweetie, just trust me. We just need to be outside for awhile." But inside I am terrified, pleading desperately with the angels to take a message to God, for it seems God can't hear me. "My world is falling apart and I don't understand it at all—please help!"

As a child growing up in the countryside near Toronto, I spent my days playing in the woods next to the creek, balancing on rocks trying to catch minnows in a glass jar, or flying around on horseback, completely free to be me. I was at one with nature, exploring and imagining my big little world. I felt, so deeply, the beauty in everything and everyone around me. *This is the divine within my heart.* I understood this as pure love, kindness and beauty—just what I found in the rest of my world, until the mirror of the world seemed to cloud and I couldn't see those things in myself anymore.

Was there something terribly wrong with me? I was often bullied, while teachers stood by and watched as if I was not worth saving. And two different times, two different men three times my age molested me. In seventh grade, I hit a wall and rarely bathed. My mom chalked it up to normal teenage angst, but now, I realize, I must have been in the grip of a full-blown depression. Something shifted inside of me as I stuffed that un-loveable little girl way down deep, keeping her there, out of sight, out of mind. I managed to create many fun adventures for years to follow, until one day I found myself in love for the very first time.

Summer, 2001. I've been with Steven for nine years. We have two beautiful children: Charlie is seven, Addie about to turn four. But I feel more alone than ever—Steven's drinking has become too much for me. Our every interaction is an inconvenience and

I understood this as pure love, kindness and beauty—just what I found in the rest of my world, until the mirror of the world seemed to cloud and I couldn't see those things in myself anymore.

annoyance to him. "How's your day looking, honey?" I ask, and he whips out his contractor's notebook and angrily rattles off each item on his to-do list at me. His dismissive attitude makes me feel I've been tossed into the dumpster, like a pair of worn-out tennis shoes. She, that unlovable little girl, bubbles up to the surface.

I'm spiraling inward, and with each clipped word from Steven, my wound expands. Then, one day, he announces he's off to Minnesota to build a house. For himself, or for all of us? It isn't clear. There's no discussion between us as a couple. He just leaves. Suddenly, I'm alone with everything—raising the kids, taking care of the house. As I try to carry on with the everyday, I find myself dissociating in the middle of the day, and feeling an unusually intense energy building inside of my belly. _What is happening to me?_

One night, two weeks after Steven has gone, my world begins to spin out of control with a velocity I've never felt before. _What are_ *these frightening memories flashing before me?* The energy building in my belly gets stronger, and I feel the presence of evil, trying to consume me, to break me down. I face this alone, with an internal courage, and try to untangle the multiple conversations screaming in my head all at once. I'm getting premonitions of the future: *Katherine, just get through this. You won't believe the magnificence on the other side.* Another voice tells me: *Your house is going to blow up. Get out now!*

Confused, exhausted and terrified, I wake up Charlie and Addie. "Children, please get up, please—you have to trust Mommy. Hurry, hurry!" I rush them outside, to the grass, to wait for the explosion—or a sign that God hears my plea for help. We wait. I am afraid to reenter the house, but my children insist that we will be okay. *I'm not going to be okay,* I think. *If our house isn't about to explode, my mind is.*

What doctors later called a psychotic episode was actually my divine awakening—my first step into enlightenment. When my walls came crashing down, I was forced to recreate me from within and find out what I was really made of.

> *I was filled with the knowing of my own soul's worth.*

While I was in the hospital, everyday miracles began to occur. Friends came out of the woodwork to support me. My spiritual teachers, whom I had yet to meet, called me to say, "We are here for you." They all were the mirrors that gave me strength. At night I imagined myself in a loving cocoon, with everything I needed to heal myself right there, inside me. I knew the divine was in my heart. In a series of little mental "films," I saw myself whole and blessed. I was filled with the knowing of my own soul's worth.

The intense energy building within my belly was actually God's energy. It was with me the whole time—my own power, emerging after years of being stuffed down away from the light. Early memories of abuse came flooding back all at once, as the little girl who had come to believe she was unlovable emerged from hiding to find her own voice. I was so clever as a little girl; I had known to put away the abuse I experienced at three until I was grown up and could handle it. I began my courageous inner journey of looking at every scary, broken part of my life to know the real truth of me. This was my time, for me.

My mother and aunt came to the hospital immediately to be with me. Steven was called back from Minnesota to care for the kids, but he refused to speak to me. I spent the first month recuperating at my mom's in Canada, and then flew back to Ogden as soon as I could. I couldn't be without Charlie and Addie for another second. I ached from missing them, and needed them to know I was okay. Since Steven was in our home and did not want me near him, I moved into a hotel and started looking for another nursing job. Though I was reluctant to take the first one I was offered, it turned out to be a huge blessing.

I had never thought of myself as someone special with elders, but we clicked. A perfect match. My residents at the skilled nursing facility made me laugh every day. Tiny Amy, an eighty-year-old Japanese lady with Alzheimer's, would whip around corners in her wheelchair holding the washcloth she'd been dusting with all day and yell, "You slept with my husband!" I would chuckle and remind her that I was the nurse, not the mistress; on she'd dust. I loved and honored my elder friends; our exchanges felt divine.

Though my days with them were filled with laughter and joy, my nights were long and painful. I cried for hours—so much I thought my heart would actually break. It had been a whole year, and Steven still refused to speak to me. I wanted reconciliation, more than anything; I wanted my family back together. I filed for divorce, thinking, *I'll wake him up and the reconciliation process can start.* Steven did come around to wanting to talk, rather than deal with my lawyer. But the happy ending I was holding out for was not to be.

Focusing on Amy and the other elders helped me stay grounded. It moved me deeply to watch Amy's husband come to the nursing home every morning with a fresh bouquet of flowers, without fail, to see her. He arranged them in a vase, pulling out the faded ones and adding the new. Then the small couple sat together quietly, sipping their coffee, as he encouraged her to eat her breakfast. By the afternoon, she would always forget he had come, but that didn't matter to him. He was happy just to be with her.

When my words changed from, "This was the worst thing that ever happened to me," to, "This is the best thing that ever happened to me," I received the gift of surrender and self-love.

Watching them mirror back was a blessing, and the timing was perfect. It reminded me what I needed from a loving relationship. *It could be harmonious and beautiful, not difficult, like for Steven and me.* Like my dad's devotion to my mom—he gave her everything he could, and he stayed near her parents all those years when he really wanted to move to Maine. They expressed their love every day, holding hands while watching TV, sneaking kisses in the kitchen. Like my grandparents—a case of love at first sight, they met at a party and were married three weeks later, and their love for each other continued to deepen.

Loving couples were all around me, mirroring what I really wanted and that a part of me never knew I was good enough to have.

Their reflection showed me that I deserved a man who would be there for me through thick and thin. My breakdown was the thick, and Steven was nowhere to be found. But then, all of the inner work I had done in my spiritual practice, and the effect of watching Mrs. Amy and her husband, came to the surface in one beautiful moment. I stood in my power and told my ex-husband, "Steven, you are one of the greatest blessings in my life because you *weren't* there for me when I needed you most."

We both laughed at the irony. "You not being there for me," I continued, "allowed me to know more of who I really am. You held up the mirror for me to see." He said, with a little sheepishness in his smile, "Thank you." I realized: *I am released.* The moment was full of the warmth and respect I'd craved so much in the days before our marriage dissolved. And here I was giving this moment *to* us. It was the only way to move forward. The exchange began a genuine friendship between us that continues today.

I know now that my breakdown was triggered by early abuse, and the trauma of Steven's withdrawal of love triggered the unaddressed feelings and experiences of a little girl who had come to believe she was unlovable. Steven was—as all our relationships are—my soul mate. He came at the right time to mirror exactly what I needed to see. It was all a part of pointing me home, to myself.

When my words changed from, "This was the worst thing that ever happened to me," to, "This is the best thing that ever happened to me," I received the gift of surrender and self-love. It was all a blessing in disguise, a chance to remember the truth I had known as a very little girl and had simply forgotten. I came into this world knowing the magnificence of who I really am: loved, lovable, loving, witty, adorable and enough, just as I am. When I forget this, my son Charlie reminds me, questioning, challenging and mirroring. I will be there to do the same for him and Addie, as the soul-foundation of a loving home that stays in one piece.

Katherine Lia began her life's work as a massage therapist and aesthetician, went on to become an RN and, later, worked in energy medicine. Her training as an intuitive life coach, ACC, certified through the NLP Institute of California, as well as her capacity to connect on a deep heart-level, has led her to become an expert in authentic relationship and transformation. Her mission is to inspire men and women in knowing their magnificent authentic power and unconditional love, and to teach them how to bring themselves in that wholeness to the dance of love. Connect with Katherine at www.Soulmate-Express.com.

Meggie Hale

The Skinny Spirit: A Quest

Our house was newish, built in the 1970s, so the stairs didn't creak when I snuck down them. It was also a pretty big house, and Dad was usually off doing something—never paying attention to me and my brothers unless he wanted to ridicule or abuse us—so even if the stairs did creak, he probably wouldn't have heard. Still, I was glad I made no noise going down them beyond my pattering footfalls. I was eleven years old.

It was night; the stove light was the only light on in the kitchen. I tiptoed to the freezer. *Please don't make any noise,* I thought, as I got ready to open it—but when I pulled the handle, *thuck!* The magnetic sucking sound went through the kitchen like a gunshot. I stood still. No sound in the house, so no one must have heard. I opened the freezer the rest of the way, and ice smoke billowed out into my face like clouds.

There it sat, so calm, so patient; my protector, my lover, my consolation, my friend: a gallon of ice cream. I grabbed the cold gallon and shut the freezer door. I scurried to the silverware drawer and opened it without making a sound. I pulled out a spoon, careful not to jingle the ones below it, and after I shut the drawer I went back up the stairs twice as fast as I'd come down. *Almost there,* I thought. I got to my bedroom, shut the door and could barely breathe. I couldn't wait.

I hid under my covers as if I had a dirty book. I took off the lid, plunged in the spoon. A huge bite: pure pleasure on my tongue. I rolled it around in my mouth, letting it melt deliciously. Then I took another bite, and another. I stopped tasting it but kept eating it. I hated this—but I loved it. I hated myself so much that I ate ice cream because it made me feel better. *You're my deepest love,* I thought, staring down at the ice cream. *And you're my greatest destroyer.*

Growing up, I had very few joys. They were limited to my Barbie dolls, being dropped off a few times at Disneyland and ice cream. Mom and Dad were divorced after my father broke almost every bone in my mother's body. She had custody of me and my brothers.

There it sat, so calm, so patient; my protector, my lover, my consolation, my friend: a gallon of ice cream.

When I was five, my father kidnapped my brothers and me, out of spite for my mother. Even at such a young age I was riddled with anxiety, because I never knew what to expect from him—a hundred dollar bill for no reason, or a severe beating, also for no reason.

Food was something I could always rely on to calm me and make me feel good, even if it was just for a few moments. As I became fatter and fatter, I became more self-conscious. Once, in the fifth grade, I was taking a math test and acing it. The questions were so easy I felt like I'd written them myself. The teacher's going to be so proud of me, I thought. Then my pencil lead broke. I sat there as horrified as if I'd peed my pants. The pencil sharpener was all the way across the room. I couldn't figure out how to get there without people looking at me. So I didn't go sharpen my pencil. And I didn't finish the test. And I failed.

But I'd come to expect failure. "You're such a failure," Dad told me constantly. He nicknamed me Stupid. "You will fail at everything you try," he told me every day. *You're right,* I always thought.

I didn't have many friends, either, and the ones I did have I couldn't bring home: Dad was interested in young girls. My mother became pregnant at fifteen; Dad was twenty-five then. He showed that same demented, disgusting interest in me once. It was at a time when I was dieting, so my weight was down. I made sure to gain weight so he would never be tempted to touch or hurt me that way again. Food not only made me feel good; it had also become my greatest protector.

The pain of being abused, taken advantage of, mocked, and mystified as to how I could possibly protect myself from more of the same left me wanting to die. I'd sit in the backyard and cut myself—miniature trial runs at suicide, practicing for the real thing. Most girls my age hung posters in their bedrooms; I hung a noose in mine. When I was thirteen, I went to my bedroom and swallowed a bunch of store-bought sleeping pills. My brother came into the room and found me half-conscious and seemingly fading into death. Hysterical, he called my father, who said in a monotone:

Food was something I could always rely on to calm me and make me feel good, even if it was just for a few moments.

"Don't worry about it." My brother walked me around for hours, holding me up, talking to me and trying to keep me from falling asleep.

By the time I was fifteen, I realized that I did not want to die; I just wanted to feel love. I was tired of my father calling me stupid, and I was tired of believing he was right. I was exhausted from living in fear and burying my emotions in food. So I decided to leave. I would lock his abuse away in a small, secure closet within my mind and visit it as seldom as possible.

I'd been working a few jobs to try to earn my own independence and find my own strength, and I had some money saved up. So one warm spring evening, I approached my father with the news. My knees shook uncontrollably; my heart felt as if it might leap out of my chest; and my mouth seemed as dry as the Sahara. I had learned early in life that the cost of speaking our minds could be much higher than either my brothers or I were prepared to pay. But now my life depended on it.

He'll scream, he'll holler, throw stuff and maybe beat me, I thought. *But I gotta give myself a chance, even if it costs me my life. I'm already dying a slow death, living like this.* I took a deep breath and went into the living room, where he was watching TV. "Dad," I said, "I want to move out." I held my breath, even winced; I waited for a beating, waited to be harangued. The blow was even harder than I had expected. It hit me like a Mack truck, right in my belly.

"Okay," was all he said. In my mind I screamed, *"What did you just say? OKAY!?! You are not going to yell, throw stuff, hit me or show me that you care even the least little bit? I'm fifteen, you jerk! I'm asking to leave your pseudo-protection and go off into the big bad world, and all you say is OKAY?!"* That hurt more than a slap across the face or a fist in my stomach. *He really doesn't care about me.*

I found an apartment for one-hundred-fifty dollars, complete with utilities, two windows and roaches, and moved in. I was both excited and scared. Once I left home, my aunt helped me secure emancipation through the school court system so that I could continue with my schooling. Eventually, I graduated from high school. It was tough being on my own, but I had escaped my father's abuse. Now all I had to do was figure out how to stop tormenting myself.

I found the supportive and loving community I had longed for, but my father had taught me well, and I had trouble receiving the love my newfound friends offered. "You're not stupid," my friends told me. "You're nice, you're smart, you're pretty, and you just graduated high school." I smiled patiently. *You just don't know the real me,* I always said in reply, but only to myself.

Now nearly one hundred and twenty pounds overweight, I battled with food, my old love and constant companion. I went on diets, lost weight, and gained it right back again. When I got my weight down, the boys came out from everywhere like *Children of the Corn*—so I knew I had attractive features. When I gained weight, it was like *The Second Coming*, they disappeared into hiding so fast. But even when I was at my thinnest, and even when I had a boyfriend, I still felt fat and alone.

After high school, I moved to California with forty dollars to my name: this was its own experiment in disaster. My loneliness became excruciating after I found myself violated again, by a man who offered me a ride. Somehow I had committed to being a lifelong victim. Heavy again and tired of all of the stares and judgmental looks, sure I would always be the stupid, ugly, fat little girl just waiting to be abused, I decided enough was enough. Since I didn't have the skills or resources to rise above my pain, since I

My "skinny" spirit was about becoming the healthy person I was born to be. And I didn't find it in a diet; I found it in the truth.

---

had lost every shred of hope and promise in my quest to break free from my need for food, I chose death instead. I shoved so many pills in my mouth that some spilled out.

Believing and accepting that I could no longer live, my last thoughts were, *I'm sorry I failed you, Meggie. I'm sorry I wasn't strong enough to beat the depression and the emptiness. You have already been dead for so long—I'm sorry I couldn't bring you back to life.* I swallowed the last pill and said goodbye.

Two days later I woke up in the ICU, tubes and wires everywhere working to keep me alive. *Damn! Why did they find me? Now I have to continue to live in this body. Now I'll never be free.* When I asked how I got there, I was told, "Your landlord found you." At first I wanted to curse her, but then I imagined her finding me, trying to revive me and calling the ambulance. In that moment, I knew I was worth saving. *You can't do that again,* I said to myself when I left the hospital. *Even a fat life is better than no life.* I resolved never to try suicide again. *You got too close to the edge, and you fell off. You let all the sadness and misery pull you in, like quicksand. Don't get near the quicksand, Meggie.*

Don't get near the quicksand. I didn't. In fact, I started running in the other direction, toward a life that I could enjoy and be proud of. With every step, I began believing in myself more. *Yes, I can take the risk and let a man love me. Yes, I can have children and raise them in a loving home.* Slowly but surely, I started to live again. Each time I felt myself slipping, I remembered that day in the hospital, and all the days I wanted to die, and pulled myself back to the land of the living.

The complete paradigm shift came at a time when I least expected it. I was taking a psychology class at a local college and decided to ask the professor for another chance at the exam, since I had been sick and unable to study. She looked at me, confused. "Meggie," she said, "you got the highest grade in the class." In that moment, I was freed. It was as if she opened a dam and the truth came rushing out. *I'm not stupid,* I thought. *My father was wrong. Why did I believe him? Maybe he was wrong about other things—maybe everything. Maybe I am nice and smart and pretty. And maybe, just maybe, I can believe in me.*

That day I found my "skinny" spirit, which, I came to realize, wasn't about being thin. My "skinny" spirit was about becoming the healthy person I was born to be. And I didn't find it in a diet; I found it in the truth. Today, the inches are peeling off to reveal the healthy body that was there all along. The once-tiny shred of belief in myself has transformed and grown into a life mission: to help others, especially teens, discover their "skinny" spirits and sculpt their bodies into healthier works of art, ones that mirror the spirits within. If I found it within me, anyone can. My true self was there all along—even under the blankets, eating a gallon of ice cream. It just took me thirty years to see it, feel it and be it.

Meggie Hale grew up eating all the wrong kinds of food—and eating a lot of them. For years, she struggled with weight and low self-esteem. After a near-fatal experience with liposuction, she spent fifteen years developing a natural mineral and body sculpting wrap system that is cost-effective, produces results and has limited risks. Over the years, she has helped thousands of clients achieve safe and substantial weight loss. Information on her product can be found at www.SlimmerSilhouette.com. Meggie's philanthropic organization offers life and food coaching; personal training; and skin, beauty and fashion consulting to teens as desperate as Meggie once was. Teens get help with setting and reaching their goals, improving their self-image and building their self-esteem. For more information, visit www.HealthyTeens.org.

Kim Warren-Martin

Shine

As the music ends, a hush sweeps the audience. I can feel my heart beating in my chest, my throat, my wrists—it's been so long since I was out there in the spotlight, shining into the dark. Now, the time has come for me to return. The auditorium is sold out, packed with hundreds of people, including several friends and colleagues who know that I am giving a welcome address. They don't know the welcome they witness tonight will be two-fold. I am also welcoming myself back from the shadows.

Though I have only three minutes to speak, it feels like I will be out there for a lifetime. And as I wait in the wings for my entrance cue, a huge lump forms in my throat, as if my heart is making its way up through my esophagus. I'm certain everyone around me can see the grapefruit-sized bulge it's causing. I struggle to maintain a calm exterior and resist the urge to gag. "Calm down," I think. "This is a safe place. You can do this! You are many years and hundreds of miles away. Even if he *is* here, he can't hurt you. You are not alone."

Several years earlier, when I competed for the title of Ms. Black Texas Metroplex, I didn't think twice about stepping out into the limelight. I welcomed it. At five-foot-one, I wasn't a typical pageant contestant, but my confidence, passion and knowledge of current events added at least nine inches to my petite frame. I had a message to share, and this pageant was tailor-made for a perfectionist like me.

I had to remember a thousand things at once during my single minute on stage as one of the top ten contestants: The content of my evening gown speech. When to say thank you. When NOT to say thank you. How to execute a perfect five-step turn around the mic in four-inch heels that killed. How to keep

---

But often at night, even with the blinds closed, I had the unnerving feeling that someone was watching me.

---

my shoulders at the right angle. And above all else—smile. Big. Lucky for me, Perfection and I were old friends…"girls," even. I had her number on speed dial under "Miss P."

At the end of the competition, the judges paid homage to Miss P's work and crowned me Ms. Black Texas Metroplex. While friends, family members and colleagues were there in spirit, Miss P was there to personally witness the moment the sparkling crown was placed on my head. Out of excitement, I cried. The photographer's pictures all bore evidence of my tears of joy. What a triumph! For both of us.

Shortly after I won the title, I moved to a new condo. It was a nice place, with a sunroom I used as an office. As a single woman, I always tried to be careful and aware of my surroundings, so I kept the mini-blinds closed at night; armed the alarm whether I was home or not; and always checked under beds, behind doors and in closets when I first got home, just as my mom taught me to do. In addition, the head of security at my job happened to live in the unit right above me. If anything happened, surely he'd help me.

But often at night, even with the blinds closed, I had the unnerving feeling that someone was watching me. Sometimes, with the hairs on my neck standing on end, I'd get up quietly from my chair, turn off the lights and peer through the blinds into the night outside. I never saw anyone, but I still felt eyes—as if the blinds were completely transparent. "Just get over it," I told myself.

One morning, I woke up with an eerie feeling and had an unusually hard time getting myself together and out the door. All day, I couldn't shake the disconcerting feeling prickling the skin on my neck and arms. Something wasn't right. I quoted scripture several times throughout the day to comfort myself. Unable to make myself just go home, I worked late, went to dinner and returned to the office to work even later.

At 1:30 a.m., I finally pulled into my lot. I walked to my condo through the courtyard, mindful of the dark corners on the way. I unlocked the door and was holding it open, ready to disarm the alarm, when I heard a male voice from behind it say, "Boo." *My dad? No. My boyfriend? No. No one has a key!* My brain rifled through a thousand explanations for the man behind the door in about one second. Nothing good surfaced. So I screamed! Screaming, I flailed my right arm in the dark toward the mysterious voice, while with my left arm I dragged my briefcase behind my back to transform it into a bludgeon.

We scuffled. I saw a flash and heard a tremendous noise—my attacker had fired a shot so close to my head that I was suddenly deaf in my left ear. I thought I had been shot. *I can't die, God! Not like this!* Then he knocked me down and ran out, probably thinking the alarm might go off at any moment. Thank God I hadn't had the chance to disarm it.

Still screaming, I clutched my head, feeling hysterically for blood. A moment later, Neal, my neighbor, came running to my door with a sawed-off shotgun (this *was* Texas). He had heard my blood-curdling screams. So had many others. In fact my neighbors made nine phone calls to 911 that night. Neal stayed with me until friends and the police arrived, reassuring me as I paced the condo, shaking and crying.

That night, my home became a crime scene wrapped in yellow tape. To my horror, police detectives said the attacker had to have been watching me. He knew my patterns, that I would come in late, and he knew the complex, because he had broken in by climbing over the patio wall, breaking into the storage room (the only room whose door was not wired to the alarm system), kicking a hole in the storage room wall and climbing into the

---

That night, my home became a crime scene wrapped in yellow tape.

---

bedroom. He made himself at home while he waited for me to arrive. He even urinated in my toilet, and vomited into one of my decorative hand towels.

The next day, my church mobilized to move me out of the condo. I never spent another night there. I put most of my things in storage and went to stay with my two college-aged sisters. For weeks, I slept on their sofa, feeling so terrified I could barely move.

My attacker was a stalker. And though he didn't succeed in raping me physically, emotionally I felt raped over and over again. A paralyzing fear had set in the moment I heard him say, "Boo—" or maybe even before that, when I felt eyes watching me through the blinds, or had my premonition: *Don't go home.* Fear began to choke the life out of me. Just walking from my car to my sisters' door was agony. I didn't know who or where he was. *What if he had followed me here? What if he tried to get to my sisters?*

My stomach became a system of knots. I dreaded nighttime. I either over-ate or under-ate, sometimes eating just to stay awake and keep watch. Often, my old friends Mountain Dew and Lay's plain potato chips would join Fear and me for an all-nighter, waiting for the sun to signal the arrival of a new day.

I created a long series of new stories, made up of what-ifs. What if I had disarmed the alarm? What if I had closed the door and turned the light on? What if he *had* shot me? I imagined him tying me up, raping me, killing me, my family's devastation.

I saw every possible outcome playing out repeatedly in my imagination.

Through all of this, I still had to complete my year as Ms. Black Texas Metroplex and was obligated to compete for the title of Ms. Black USA Metroplex. What I wanted most was to crawl into a cave and seal it from the inside. Somehow, I felt this would give me back control of my life.

Through many moments of intense fear and inexpressible mental torture, I went on to fulfill my obligations as Ms. Black Texas Metroplex and even won the next title. But every day my mind experienced the attack as if it had happened only yesterday. The thought of making public appearances for another year nauseated me. What if he was there, waiting, watching? Crippled with fear, I resigned my new title one month later.

To fulfill my contract, I took the title back after a few weeks. But the moment I crowned the next Ms. Black USA Metroplex, I retreated from the spotlight. Terror had me on a chain in a cold, dark, unnatural place. While doing time there, memories

---

What I wanted most was to crawl into a cave and seal it from the inside. Somehow, I felt this would give me back control of my life.

---

of my past liberty gave me hope and strength to scratch and fight my way back. Though I had many sleepless nights, I learned to live alone again. With jagged nails and bleeding fingers, I even bought a home. It was a hard uphill battle to get to the place in the wings where I stand right now, waiting for the emcee to cue my entrance.

Dressed in red, I symbolize the torture, pain and fear I felt for so long—while honoring the power and faith I gained from my struggle. Breathing deeply, settling my heart back into my chest, I remember that the attack was a blessing, though not what I would have asked for had I made a request—an opportunity to journey back to fearlessness and let my story help others conquer fear. I can do all things through Christ, who strengthens me. And I know it is time to emerge again, into the light that's mine. *"Please help me welcome to the stage, Mrs. Kim Warren-Martin."* I'm no longer afraid of my own light—I'm ready to shine!

Kim Warren-Martin is passionate about helping others free themselves from the traps of fear and perfectionism. She is a speaker, actress, playwright and the author of a forthcoming book inviting others on a journey to overcome trauma and step into the spotlight. Connect with Kim at www. KimWarrenMartin.com.

Pamela V. Bell

For the Kids

Labor Day that year was hot. The temperature was high, but there was no breeze, which was unusual. My friend, Barbara, who was hosting the barbecue, lived close enough to Lake Michigan to catch some lake effect breeze. Not that day. Even sitting in the shade didn't bring much relief.

All the other parents were delighted when Michael volunteered to take the kids for ice cream, but I was skeptical. Barbara was my co-worker, and Michael was a friend of her friend, so I didn't know him from Adam. He was tall, he was quite good looking; it was obvious he could afford the finer things. But still, I didn't know him.

"It's okay," one of the other parents said to me. "Michael's a good guy." He had been playing with the kids all afternoon. Plus, I was tired. I was a single parent with a four year-old daughter, a six year-old son and another daughter who visited me occasionally. I had a full-time job and was going to school—and life was wearing me out. Someone taking my kids for a couple of hours was heaven. My friends trusted Michael, so I operated on their trust. He came back two hours later. The kids were happy, and my nerves were settled.

Michael and I both worked in downtown Chicago, and a month after that Labor Day when we first met, we got together for lunch.

He was easy to talk to; he was smooth. I liked him. Over the months, we met a few more times for coffee or lunch, and then in March, on a nasty, cold, rainy night, we had our first date. He took me to an expensive restaurant, and I felt like a queen. It had been so long since I'd felt special. I'd divorced my husband a year before, and at the time I was so low—emotionally, financially, spiritually—that

> *So for all the wrong reasons, some might say,*
> *I allowed Michael to move in. I cared for him,*
> *but I knew the reason I let him into my home*
> *was the financial security he brought along.*

I had agreed to let him have our baby daughter without any fight. But being with Michael lifted my spirits. I felt, for the first time in a long time, like a lady again. I wasn't sure if Michael was great or if my self-esteem was so low that I made him great; but either way, I was along for the ride.

A couple of weeks later, Michael and I took my two kids out for burgers. Before dinner, my son reached for the salt shaker. "Don't touch that," Michael said sharply. My son, confused, kept quiet. During dinner, my son stood up to grab one of his sister's fries, and Michael snapped, "Sit down." "That's a little harsh," I said, and he replied, "They need to be trained." *Did he just say "trained,"* I thought? But as I chewed my food, I figured that though "trained" wasn't the best word, maybe my kids did need a little more structure.

Sleeping by myself every night took its toll, but not nearly so much as my constant worry about how I would feed my kids and keep them warm. *Maybe if I buy noodles and rice again, we can cut up two pieces of chicken and make it go further. Maybe if I buy new hats and gloves, their worn-out coats will be enough to get them through those zero-degree days with the wind loud as a stereo.* I was tired of suffering, and being afraid that one day everything would run out, making me the mother of two starving, freezing children. So for all the wrong reasons, some might say, I allowed Michael to move in. I cared for him, but I knew the reason I let him into my home was the financial security he brought along.

Soon enough, Michael's verbal abuse moved like thunder through the house, leaving everyone shaken and afraid. "You are a bad and hard-headed little boy," he'd yell at my son, "and you will NEVER amount to anything in life." My son waited until Michael left the house before he told me the most heartbreaking news: "Mommy, when you're not here, Michael beats me with his fists and yanks my arms so hard." I confronted Michael, and he said, "If he behaved, I wouldn't have to spank him." "How did he misbehave?" I asked. "He stole from me." I asked my son if he was stealing, and he nodded yes, tears running down his cheeks.

I sat quietly, wondering if my child was okay, flinching as I imagined the beating he must have gotten to have Child Protective Services called in. In that moment, I did not know who I hated more—Michael or myself.

I had a huge problem with the abuse, but I didn't know how to get out of it and be able to feed and clothe my children. Stealing had become a problem for my son. He was very frustrated with Michael, so he channeled his anger into taking toys from other kids, money from wallets. In my own unwillingness to choose between Michael and a life of precarious poverty, I chose to believe that the problem was my son's stealing.

My world came crashing down one night when I went to my babysitter's house to pick up my children. She said that someone had already taken them. My heart jumped. "Who?" I asked. "The state authorities. Their principal at school found bruises on your son's back and he called it in."

Someone hold the room still, I thought. I felt as if my legs would quit working, and nothing would hold me up. Ashamed, infuriated and scared, I raced back to the car where Michael was waiting to take us all home.

I glared at the man that I had allowed to come into my home and change everything. "What did you do to him?" I asked. "I found a letter he'd written," Michael said, "and it had profanity. When I asked him about it, he lied and said he didn't write it. So I took a belt to him." My stomach was flipping, my head was spinning and my heart was shattering into a thousand pieces. I sat quietly, wondering if my child was okay, flinching as I imagined the beating he must have gotten to have Child Protective Services called in. In that moment, I did not know who I hated more—Michael or myself.

We arrived at the facility where my son was being kept. The authorities made Michael wait in the lobby. My heart beat irregularly. It was the heartbeat of a woman who had lost control of her life, and whose children now paid the price. When my son and I saw each other, we ran to each other with tear-filled eyes.

Afraid of what I might see, I pulled up his shirt and almost vomited. Black, purple and blue welts and gashes laced my beautiful son's back. I would not have any mercy for the mother who allowed her children to be beaten by a live-in boyfriend; I

Not sure I deserved it, I asked him, "Do you forgive me?" I held my breath, waiting for him to laugh in my face, but he said, "Yes, Mommy, I forgive you." Because of my own guilt, I never felt sure of his answer.

---

would recommend that they take the children away from her until she found her senses. But with what happened next, I proved that I *had* lost all of my sense. I could only see my son for a few minutes, but I told him I'd do everything I could to get him back. And I did do everything, everything to bring the next block of chaos and trauma crashing down on me.

Our caseworker told me that I stood a better chance of getting my children back if Michael were my husband and not just a boyfriend. *I can't believe that I am even entertaining the idea of marrying this man.* But as every day passed and my son was not in our home, a piece of me died away. I married Michael, and when I said, "I do," I heard a jail cell door slam and lock me into my own personal prison. But I kept lying to myself. *I can make it work,* I thought. *When the kids come home I will work extra hard to keep peace and order, and what happened before will never happen again.*

I became pregnant with Michael's baby. I was excited to give birth but worried about my newborn baby and how his father would treat him. From day one with Landon, I was amazed by Michael's behavior with him. There was no temper, no anger, no abuse, nothing. I couldn't believe this was the same man who had been so terrible to my son. Together, they were exactly what a father and son should be.

I fought like hell to get my other children back. I went to court, I took special classes, I appealed to authorities. It was an uphill battle that took two years, but eventually my children came home. The only thing I thought about was my son's forgiveness. My daughter had already told me she'd forgiven me. Not sure I deserved it, I asked him, "Do you forgive me?" I held my breath, waiting for him to laugh in my face, but he said, "Yes, Mommy, I forgive you." Because of my own guilt, I never felt sure of his answer.

With everyone back but my baby girl, I fought for custody of her, too. And after nine years of fighting, I won. A few years ago, I took my youngest daughter to a birthday party. While there, I ran into a man who spoke about his relationship with his mother and his stepfather, whom she'd married when this man was just a young boy. "I hated my stepfather," he said, and I felt the venom seeping from his lips as he spoke. "He used to beat me and beat me. To this day, I can't even visit my mother because they're still married."

I felt emotionally naked. This man had just told my son's story, and could well have been telling my future with my son. Soon after the party, I began the process of divorcing Michael. Michael fought the divorce, claiming I would be much better off with him. "I have made enough decisions out of fear and lack, and I am making this decision from a place of power and clarity," I told him. I was late in getting the message and the courage to move, but once I had them, there was no turning back. All I cared about was my son.

I spent years pouring back into my empty tank, filling myself up with life, self-esteem, and self-love. I became comfortable and confident being alone. I learned how to stand on my spiritual and emotional prosperity. My forgiveness for myself is a work in progress, but I'm more concerned with the forgiveness of my children. Some days I still expected my son to blot my name from his memory because of what I had subjected him to. But one afternoon a few years back, he came over to my new house with a mischievous smile on his face. I asked, "What are you smiling about?" He didn't say a word, just pulled up his T-shirt—and there, tattooed across his chest in stunning black letters, was the most beautiful declaration of forgiveness I had ever seen: my name, Pamela. In that moment, I took my first breath in ten years.

Pamela V. Bell is a social entrepreneur, child advocate and mother. In 2001, Pamela co-founded an information-consulting firm specializing in the development of customized software lifecycle processes for the banking, retail, insurance, health care and government sectors. For more than ten years, Pamela has also been a tireless advocate for women and children. She serves as a CASA, advocating for abused and neglected children, and in 2008 she was selected to serve on the board of the CASA Foundation. In addition to running the lucrative marketing company she opened last year, Pamela devotes her life to fighting for kids and encouraging the global community to help support and assist single parents. Her book, Kid Connection, *helps empower people to be better parents in today's challenging culture. Connect with Pamela Bell at www.PamelaVBell.com.*

M. Bridget Cook

Learning to Dance in the Rain

The cloud of white-hot fever lifted briefly, but it was only a matter of time before it invaded my body again with its earth-shattering ache, its debilitating nausea. Pierced as it was, I tried to hear my heart inside my chest. The wires and tubes were only faintly visible in the dim light from the hospital corridor.

"Should we call her mother?" whispered one nurse, just outside my door. The other sighed heavily. "We might have to," she said, simply. "I don't think she is going to make it until morning." Their words tore into me, but I had no fight left. Off and on, I could feel myself slipping away... I wasn't going home.

Just a few days before, I had finally surrendered to the devastating infection raging through my body. I deserted classes and jobs to seek help from my mother. How I longed to be a child wrapped in her arms, feeling no judgment, no expectations—simply loved. It didn't matter that I had been away at college for a few years. All I wanted was for my mother to put me to bed like a child and make me well again. *Sleep. Just sleep—forever. Maybe all my troubles will disappear by the time I wake up—if I wake up.*

I couldn't remember the drive through the treacherous canyon or the quiet streets leading to the warm familiarity of home. As I pushed weakly through the door, my mother's look of greeting changed to instant alarm. She immediately whisked me into the car and across town to the doctor's office, where I collapsed. *What was happening?*

I was helpless as they rushed me to the hospital and into emergency surgery, where they discovered seriously diseased tissue and pumped out pint after pint of infection. It should have worked, the surgery, the intravenous antibiotics—so many of them—fighting the infection that was attacking my body. But nothing was working, and no one knew why.

"You know you're going to die, don't you?" asked my roommate, the woman whom I had befriended between my raging fevers. The woman who had endured intensive gallbladder surgery, but was brought back writhing in pain because her body wouldn't accept

---

Sleep. Just sleep—forever. Maybe all my troubles will disappear by the time I wake up—if I wake up.

---

medication. The one who could feel every slice of the scalpel, every agonizing stitch. The one I heard, behind a closed curtain, experience the healing miracle of a blessing. The same one who had then sighed and fallen peacefully asleep less than fifteen seconds later.

"Yes," I answered hesitantly. *What else was there to say?* Gone were the pretty stories and excuses for my behavior. Facing the thought of death, I took an honest look at myself and was horrified by what I saw. Hot tears of shame and regret streamed down my cheeks for my disastrous choices: substance abuse, lies and co-dependency, with ruined relationships hovering all around my existence. *What happens after my heart stops beating?* I believed in an afterlife—at least, I had been raised to believe in heaven. Then again, there was also that *other* place. The one where sinners go. The one where I was sure that I was headed.

I wondered if I had been living at all. *What had I done?* Lived for the approval of others. Snapshots flashed into my consciousness: my parents, young and in college, pressured to give me up for adoption. Foster parents who cared for me until I was six months old. I was finally placed with amazing adoptive parents—but always wondered when they were going to leave, too. *Wasn't I pretty enough? Wasn't I smart or good enough for my birth parents to want to keep me?* As a little girl I asked my mother these questions, and saw the pain in her eyes. She couldn't tell me, but I had to know what I did *wrong*. I ended up creating behaviors to overcome my "wrongness." One was to do everything for myself! Dress myself, tie my own shoes, work three jobs and go to school. Forget the joy and the dance of life. Work, work, work and prove, prove, prove that I was good enough to be chosen. That's why I ended up half-dead in this hospital room.

My self-sabotaging behavior was so ugly I could hardly look at it. But in my surrender, I realized that if there was ever a time to be radically truthful, it was now. *Be honest, Bridge... you've been looking for someone to love you in every person you've ever met!*

My heart felt as if someone had ripped it from my chest. I would never be able to say "I'm sorry," or "I love you" to my parents. I would never fall in love again. I would never marry. I would never have children.

Seeking to please your parents, bosses, friends—even strangers. When was the last time you had any shred of what you want out of life? Any idea of who YOU are?

I wanted to scream at God, but I didn't think he would hear me. The room was cold, the only warmth coming from the woman behind the curtain and the memory of Mom's presence from hours before. She had stayed by my side for two days, and even Dad had come to visit after a long day of work. I could see their worried faces, and knew that they had been praying fervently even after going home exhausted. *All of the pain I have put them through, and they still love me this much? They still accept me?* I could hardly fathom that, in my fear of abandonment, I had snubbed the very thing I had been craving: unconditional love.

My heart felt as if someone had ripped it from my chest. I would never be able to say "I'm sorry," or "I love you" to my parents. I would never fall in love again. I would never marry. I would never have children. I was shocked by this truth; my tears stopped and a quiet stillness came over me. *God, could you please send me a miracle?* I even asked for a blessing like the one I had heard beyond that curtain, with that woman. *Could anyone have one of those blessings?* I had asked, then—*Really? Even someone like me?*

I woke from another fever to find I was being ministered to by two loving strangers. It seemed ironic that I had nothing to offer them—nothing to give them or with which to please them. But in the moment, I embraced the love of these two strangers, their warm, soft hands on my head… and it was the gateway, the opening to the love that my parents had always offered me and the love that rippled out to me through their prayers. I even surrendered, finally, to the love of God.

Suddenly, I felt virtually *wrapped* in the most tender embrace that I had ever experienced, though no one was actually touching me physically. It was beyond comprehension—*greater, even, than a parent's love!* It was a universal love. The dismal, negative cloud had lifted, and I could see that the entire room was filled with the sweetest presence, one I would remember forever. In my lowest of lows, this love poured out onto me like rainwater quenching a thirsty soul, washing through me—*washing me*. It was so cleansing and healing that I fell sound asleep in its loving arms, with the promise of a new life.

When I awoke, I was completely coherent—and inexplicably excited! A second chance at LIFE! I gasped as now-familiar waves of unconditional love washed through me, and felt an unspeakable fire within—only this time, it wasn't a raging fever! When the nurse wheeled in another series of intravenous antibiotics, I pointed to the one wrapped in foil. It was so familiar to me, as if I could see its every molecule, its good intentions—and its thoroughly devastating consequences.

"I-CANNOT-HAVE-THAT-ONE," I blurted to my nurse, each syllable spoken with serious deliberation. "What?" she exclaimed at my outburst. "You *must* have all of these antibiotics. They're the only thing saving your life!" "No!" I persisted, amazed at my own clarity and conviction, regardless of her dissatisfaction with me. "This one is *killing* me! I refuse to take it into my body."

I had fallen in love with the possibilities of the human soul, and it spilled out into pages of true stories of challenges and triumph. My writing became as authentic and magical as the people it illustrated.

The nurse gave me a dubious look and hurried away to find the doctor. "I can't explain it," I said to him. "I just KNOW." Joy filled my heart when my doctor agreed to experiment for a few hours while monitoring my fragile condition. It began to improve so dramatically in that short time that he and the staff finally agreed: I must have been intensely allergic to the specific antibiotic I had refused.

Amazed at my quick and thorough recovery, the doctor asked, "Do you have *any* idea what happened to you in the last twenty-four hours?" He peered intently into my eyes after he had glanced through my chart several times. A look passed between us—we were witnesses to a miracle, acknowledgers of the mysterious love of God. It was unbelievable, and yet, here I was. Even the next shift of nurses stared wide-eyed as I stepped away from the hospital and into the arms of my parents and my new life.

The next night in my college apartment bathroom, I gazed into my reflection. I was amazed to see evidence of the change in my face, particularly in my eyes. Where once only the living dead stared back at me, now there was pure light and joy! *How long have I waited, burdened and impatient, for all my storms to subside so I could taste the promise of a rainbow?* With perfect clarity, I realized that such a moment would *never* come. *Life is not about waiting for all the storms to pass—it is about dancing in the rain!*

I began to embrace the world and my place in it, no longer bent on trying to please—just loving. It happened, sometimes in baby steps. After marrying and graduating college, I moved to Denver with my husband and the first of our three beautiful, miraculous children (whom we were told we would never have). Through my work as writer and publicist for Community Learning Centers, I worked directly with high-risk, often gang-related, youth.

Despite their frequently horrendous histories, from time to time some claimed accountability for their own choices. What I witnessed then was transformation: kids who took the same step that I had, and pledged to become the captains of their own souls. The new light in their eyes became fiery sparks of commitment to do life differently... from utter darkness to beautiful illumination. I had fallen in love with the possibilities of the human soul, and it spilled out into pages of true stories of challenges and triumph. My writing became as authentic and magical as the people it illustrated.

Mother Teresa said, "I am the pen in the hand of a God who is writing a love letter to the world." *That's me!* Though I am no Mother Teresa, my light has *purpose.* The love I will remember forever has translated into writing the most unusual true stories of transformation—"Samaritan stories" that most writers would recoil from examining too closely. Because I faced my greatest darkness in that hospital room, and in my own soul, I can now write compassionately about the journeys of others. Today I am the pen of a loving God. I write—and teach—of courageous souls who don't wait for the storms to pass, but choose to dance in the rain.

M. Bridget Cook is a national bestselling author, transformational speaker and success coach. Awed by the extremes of human behavior, she wrote Shattered Silence: The Untold Story of a Serial Killer's Daughter *(Sweetwater Books, Cedar Fort 2009) with Melissa G. Moore, daughter of the infamous Happy Face serial murderer, and* Skinhead Confessions: From Hate to Hope *(Sweetwater Books, Cedar Fort 2009) with former high-ranking neo-Nazi skinhead leader T. J. Leyden. Her books have been featured on* Oprah, Dr. Phil, Good Morning America, 20/20, *CNN,* NPR, *and in* People Magazine, In-Touch *and other publications. In her forthcoming book,* The Magic and Miracle of Living Your Life On Purpose, *Bridget teaches that you have the ability to create miracles through the magic of gratitude and contribution— by commandeering your life with the magnificent power of vision. Connect with Bridget at www.MBridgetCook.com.*

Lisa Nichols

Conclusion

L et me start by saying that I am no one's guru. I'm simply an ordinary woman who, like the co-authors in this book, chose to make extraordinary decisions. That's it. When you demystify success and stop making it about magic or something unattainable, it becomes available for everyone. These co-authors have triumphed over adversity, but they aren't better, stronger, smarter or more courageous than you. They are just like you. Their triumphs are *your* triumphs.

> *And I hope that, as you celebrate the co-authors in this book, you recognize that you are the author of your own story as well.*

I hope that, in reading the transformational true stories in this book, you not only allowed yourself to meet more than thirty-five great friends; but that in one, two or more of these stories you found your own power and conviction, your choice to get back up, your choice to love again, your choice to believe again. I hope you were inspired by these stories, and also inspired by your own story and who you have become. And I hope that, as you celebrate the co-authors in this book, you recognize that you are the author of your own story as well.

You may not yet know exactly the story you would share with us, but you do *have* a story. Keep in mind that though your chapters one through twenty-three may already be set in stone and you can't change the story of your past, your chapter twenty-four is still *waiting* to be written.

If your chapter four was filled with disappointment or fear, it does not equal your chapter twenty-four. I invite you to join our community at www.Lisa-Nichols.com and get the free gift I have prepared for you. And remember, no one can take your destiny from you...so get up, shake off your limiting beliefs and rise up to grab it!

I'm your sister in the journey!

About Lisa Nichols

Lisa Nichols, the "Breakthrough Specialist," has reached millions around the world with her powerful message of empowerment, service, excellence and gratitude. Founder of Motivating the Masses and CEO of Motivating Teen Spirit, LLC, Lisa is a charismatic teacher, speaker and transformational coach. Featured in the self-development phenomenon, *The Secret,* she has appeared on *The Oprah Winfrey Show, Larry King Live* and on NBC's Emmy award-winning reality show, *Starting Over.*

Lisa co-authored *Chicken Soup for the African American Soul* and *Chicken Soup for the African American Woman's Soul.* Her book *No Matter What!: 9 Steps to Living the Life You Love* hit six bestseller lists, including *The New York Times,* and has been translated into twenty-five languages. Lisa has been honored with many awards for her empowering work, including the Humanitarian Award from South Africa. Connect with Lisa at www.Lisa-Nichols.com.

We invite you to experience the
Living Proof MULTIMEDIA book.

Now that you've read these moving stories, you can also view the online version of LIVING PROOF on your computer or iPad in an exciting, next-generation multimedia format.

Adding AUDIO and VIDEO conversations to the text, the co-authors share more knowledge and inspiration to help you become the champion of your own life.

We offer you a GIFT of several chapters from the *Living Proof* multimedia book at:

www.LivingProofMBook.com

If you wish to buy the complete multimedia book, please use this coupon code to receive a substantial discount.

Coupon Code — Book5

Truths that Build

Dick Iverson's book, Truths that Build, *is a blending of biblical truth and practical wisdom. This book will not only bless you, but it will encourage you to build your life and ministry around biblical principles of personal and corporate growth. Do you want to grow a healthy church? Read this book!*

Joe Aldrich
President Emeritus, Multnomah Bible College and Seminary, Portland Oregon

Pastor Dick Iverson's life message is definitely the glorious church of Jesus Christ. Anytime he turns his pen towards this subject it is worthy to listen carefully and once again, he has given us a rich harvest of wisdom in Truths that Build. *I have seen these truths in action in his personal life and ministry and recommend this book to all who desire to build wisely.*

Mike Herron
Salem, Oregon

Dick Iverson has drawn from his rich experience to present "time-tested" and "biblically-based" principles. It goes beyond style and methods to offer eternal truth that can be expressed in the local church. Bro. Iverson writes as he has lived; He presents solid thought in useful form. And like his ministry, his message endures.

Charles Simpson, Chairman of CSM Publishing
Mobile, Alabama

Brother Dick Iverson is a spiritual father to many people and is known for his practical and biblically sound truths that work in any believer's life and in any culture. This book reflects his 50 years' experience of teaching, preaching, and nurturing people to make wise life decisions that build a fruitful Christian life.

Frank Damazio
Senior Pastor, City Bible Church, Portland Oregon

There is no doubt about the fact that "truth is timeless." Truth is truth in every generation. What was truth yesterday was truth several thousand years ago. What was truth then is truth now. This is why Bro. Dick Iverson's new book Truths that Build *is so relevant for today. I have no hesitation in recommending this text to all ministers of the Gospel. Brother Dick has ministered these same truths over many, many years. Though often repeated, they still have the same transforming and releasing power as ever. "Know the truth and the truth sets you free" – free from traditions that are contrary to Scripture, free from many religious "hangups" that rob God's people in our generation. These truths, wherever preached and practiced have built churches that last!*

Kevin J. Conner
MFI National Leader – Australia

I've learned a great deal over the years from the life and ministry of Dick Iverson, one of city's esteemed fathers-in-the-faith and pastor of pastors. In the midst of these perilous and opportune days, I hope we all embrace Dick's message to the Church of Jesus Christ: our growth and impact have little to do with style and technique, but everything to do with substance and strengthening our grip on timeless, foundational, and oft-neglected truths of God's Word.

Dr. Ron Mehl, Pastor
Beaverton Foursquare Church, Beaverton, Oregon

To Laurel Lee

My spiritual Daughter in the Lord

Thank you for your life testimony

You shall live on ~~you~~ when you are with Jesus

Ps 27

Love,
Dick Iverson